THANKS AMERICA - YOU SET ME FREE

by

ULLA REICHHARDT

Bloomington, IN   authorHouse™   Milton Keynes, UK

AuthorHouse™
1663 Liberty Drive, Suite 200
Bloomington, IN 47403
www.authorhouse.com
Phone: 1-800-839-8640

AuthorHouse™ UK Ltd.
500 Avebury Boulevard
Central Milton Keynes, MK9 2BE
www.authorhouse.co.uk
Phone: 08001974150

First published by AuthorHouse   5/23/2006

ISBN: 1-4259-3691-1 (sc)

Library of Congress Control Number: 2006904441

Printed in the United States of America
Bloomington, Indiana

This book is printed on acid-free paper.

Introduction

Who am I? What is my destiny? Why am I here on earth?

All these questions were on my mind from my early childhood on. I always wanted to know more about my purpose in being here. Looking back, I see that everything I lived through and did was meant to be. There is a higher Spirit who helps me to look inside of me… Who shows me my purpose of being here on earth? I realize that I learned so much and changed a lot during all those years. From a shy and tied-up child, I grew to accept myself and be myself. But I am still working on it.

What really helped me to overcome my anxiety were a lot of happenings or events. But one of the greatest was to move to America, where I was able to become myself. The freedom in this country to be yourself without being judged for everything made me free to grow.

Thank you, America!

The first years of my childhood I remember are those horrible years of World War II. As a child, I recall that there were alarms every night, and then we had to rush into a bunker, because bombs were falling. There were so-called "Christmas trees" made of fireworks set for the area which was supposed to be bombed. Night after night, we rushed first into a cellar and later into a bunker. I remember I prayed to God, "Please give me one night to sleep through," but it did not happen. One time, a bomb fell very close by, and my mother jumped up, holding her arms up in front of me to protect me. My father was gone; he was a soldier in the war.

One day, my mother brought me to my nursery school. I must have been five years old. All of a sudden, she said: "This Hitler…now he takes all crucifixes out of the schools. He is bad." Then she looked at me, very distraught, and added: "Oh, God, please, never ever tell anybody what I just said, because I will be killed." I did not know what she was talking about, but I knew one thing: that I never would mention this to any human person.

I did a very bad thing which I will remember forever. In 1942, my father was discharged from the army because he was too old. He came home. I was playing in the street with my friends, when all of a sudden I saw my daddy coming from the station. I yelled, "Daddy, Daddy!" and started to run towards him.

My friends looked at me and said, "That fat man is your father?"

I turned around and told them, "No, that is not my father." He must have been very hurt, because I heard this story over and over again when I was growing up.

In 1943, all schoolchildren were evacuated with their whole schools into rural areas, because we lived in an industrial region. Only the teacher came along, but no parents. My mother did not want to let me go alone with my school, so we went to the Black Forest, where my aunt was vacationing with my cousins. First we lived in Hotel Zum Schwanen for a couple of months, till we found an apartment. Every day, we ate in the restaurant, and I had to learn how to eat correctly with a fork and knife. I was so thrilled when I got praised; therefore, I watched my table manners carefully. After a couple of months, we rented two rooms from a lady whose husband was killed in the war. She had three children.

My mother was Catholic, my father of Lutheran faith. I was raised in the Catholic Church. Everybody in this little village in the Black Forest was Catholic, and so was our landlord. I had to go to church every morning. One day, I was wearing my favorite sweater. It was handmade by an aunt and showed people dancing. One child came to me and told me, "How can you wear something like that? We have a war and nobody is allowed to dance. Shame on you!" I was shocked and never ever did wear that sweater again.

Sunday mass was the highlight of the week. We had a pastor who meant serious business. If somebody laughed, he shouted at that person from the pulpit. Once, he came down from his pulpit during the sermon and hit a child who didn't behave. I was so afraid of him and did everything I was asked to do.

I do recall Christmas 1943. We had nothing to eat, yet it was the greatest Christmas I can remember. At midnight, we went to church on our skis. The village was surrounded by mountains, tugged into the woods. The church in the middle of the town was lit up beautifully. From all around, people on skis came down the mountains with little lanterns. It looked like blinking stars falling down from the skies upon the church, where a big light was to be seen. The next morning we exchanged gifts.

That's what we did. I and all the other children believed that the Christ child came at night with his angels and brought all the gifts. The angels had made all the toys, and baked cookies and Christmas stollen in heaven. I actually could see it on earth when they were baking. It was around sunset when the heavens were red. The oven in heaven was so hot that we were able to see it on earth. This is what little children believe in Germany. There is no Santa, but a St. Nikolaus. We celebrate on December 6, his birthday. St. Nikolaus is the Christ child's helper. He goes with his helper, Knight Ruprecht, on this day from house to house and checks out the children. He will report everything to the Christ child. Some are good, and some are bad. He knows them all. The good ones get candies, cookies, and chocolate that day. The naughty ones Knecht Ruprecht, or Knight Ruprecht, spanks and carries them away in a big sack to be punished. I experienced this when both visited us. We all gathered at my aunt's house with two other families. We children were very excited and a little bit afraid. Had I been good or bad? Then the two came. I was very nervous. Had I really been good? Yes, I got candies, but one big boy who always liked to fight with us small children got no candies and was carried away. I felt sorry for him. Now I knew one thing: the Christ child would bring me something, and I was looking forward to Christmas.

I still recall when I learned the truth that there was no Christ child who brought us all the gifts and the Christmas tree. It was Christ's birthday that we celebrated on December twenty-fifth, and the parents bought or made the gifts, decorated the home, and bought the Christmas tree. I did not believe in anything anymore and was so disappointed. My parents had lied to me, and all the books I read about the Christ child and the angels were not true either.

But in 1943, I still believed in the Christ child and all the angels who brought us gifts. We were poor, but on Christmas Day my doll got beautiful new clothes. My mother had sewed those during many nights when I was asleep. A little Christmas tree was lit up in the corner, and a beautiful Christmas plate was filled with homemade cookies, apples, and nuts. Before I was allowed to look at the goodies, we sang Christmas songs, and I had to say a Christmas poem by heart. I had learned it for this day, and Mother read from the Bible the Christmas story of when Christ was born. Then I was allowed to discover all the gifts. There was no chocolate. I remembered that only twice in my life I had eaten a little piece of chocolate. It was war, and those items were not available. My mother told me that before the war, she was able to buy chocolate as much as she wanted. I looked at her stomach and thought to myself, "Lucky stomach! All the chocolate must be in it."

The lady we rented our rooms from had us over after "Bescherung" (exchanging of the gifts) to show us a surprise. In her living room was a huge manger made out of wood. It covered almost the whole room. Her husband was a carpenter and had made this before the war. The figures of Josef and Mary were at least 3 feet tall. It was overwhelming, and I still picture this beautiful manger today. After we admired the manger, we sang more Christmas carols: "Silent night," "O Christmas Tree."

I do not recall our dinner anymore. Usually the main dish is a goose. I do not know if we were able to afford this. But I do remember a beautiful cake Mother made. It was a Black Forest cake.

After Christmas, we went back home by train to see my father. He was working and was not able to be with us. After a couple of hours, when the train stopped in one big city, there was an air-raid. The sirens were going on and off, which marked the beginning. My mother panicked, grabbed me, and wanted to get out off the train, but the conductor closed the doors and told us, "The train is leaving this station, and nobody can get off." All the lights were turned off in the train, and we were riding back and forth outside of that city. There was a dead silence all around us. We saw the "Christmas trees" set over the city. We heard the bombs falling, and the sky was illuminated. The houses were burning. We all had to lie down on the floor of the train. I was at the end of all the people, and nobody was around my legs. I still remember how afraid I was that my legs would get hit. We survived, but if we had left the train, we would have been dead. That city—it was Stuttgart—had the worst air-raid ever, and the station was destroyed totally. Our guardian angel saved us. He saved us the second time on this trip. Originally we intended to take another train earlier, but my mother overslept. That train had a terrible accident, and most of the people got killed.

Being Catholic, I always prayed to God. It was a sin not to pray, and I had to go to confession if I did not pray. I was afraid to forget to pray, because then I would be punished. Sometimes I did ten prayers all at once in case I forgot it; then I was on the sure side and had some extra. I was very much afraid that I would have to go to hell. I went constantly to confession. At one point, I started to pray for something for myself. I was an only child, and I wanted a brother or sister. I prayed and prayed. God listened. In 1944, my sister was born. I was so happy and thought she is the nicest baby on earth. But I never thought that I had scores to do. Every day I had to push her carriage and go for a walk with her. At first I liked it very much, but then it became a drag. I had had it! So I prayed to God again: "God, you can have her back. It is too much work." This time he did not listen. I am grateful for that.

After one year, the Black Forest was not safe anymore. The battlefield came closer and closer. My mother, my sister, and I went to the heart of Germany, "Thueringen," where my parents thought we would be safe. During this time, I saw people whispering and very afraid, looking around to see if anybody could hear them. I never found out what they were talking about, but today I believe it was about the concentration camps, which must have become known. We were in Thueringen when the war ended and the American soldiers moved in and occupied the whole area. At first I was very afraid, because they were the enemies; but when I saw they did not harm us, I overcame my fear. I had never seen or eaten a banana. When we children played ball in the street, some soldier came by and gave us one. This was the first banana I had ever eaten. A black soldier gave us cookies. I never before had seen a black person. It was very interesting, and I liked those soldiers more and more. They even played with us. I recall that we children went to their camp and picked up brewed coffee, which was not available during the war, for the adults.

Soon we were able to move back to our town. Our house was not bombed. We were lucky. I went to a Catholic school again after having been out of school for one year. All schools were closed at the end of the war. Once again, I had to go to church every morning. In school we started with a prayer. I felt so sorry for all sinners. My own father never went to church on Sunday; that was a big sin. I prayed for him.

My best girlfriend was Margarete. We were together every day. We did nice and bad things together. "Bad" was…we smoked our first cigarette together. She stole one from her father. We had a little window in our pantry. This we opened and took turns blowing the smoke out of the window. Afterwards, I recall I got dizzy. Margarete had two big brothers. I envied her. They always could protect her. Her father had a painting business. They got rich fast after the war and were the first who owned a car. Margarete and I took a lot of photos of it. First she was sitting at the steering-wheel and then I. I promised myself to get rich and get a car.

In 1947, I had my first communion. My mother had damask fabric lying around from before the war for my white communion dress, which she sewed herself. The war was over, but we all were still poor. Every day we ate turnips cooked in water or barley soup. After church in the morning, I had a piece of dry bread toasted on the stove with nothing on it. My communion day, March 17, 1946, was my highlight. I felt like an angel because I had confessed all my sins, and now Jesus came to me. On my communion photo, taken by a photographer, I tried not to smile. I was happy and wanted to; but in the Black Forest I had learned it was a sin to smile on your communion-photo, and I wanted to send one of the photos over to our friends. So I forced myself to look very serious. I got gifts.

The most memorable one was a bag of potatoes, because they were hard to get.

One thing I learned as a child which I still like today. Every Sunday, my father went hiking through the woods for a couple of hours. I loved to go with him, because we talked about everything. At the end of this walk or hike, we went to a restaurant, and I got an apple cider and an open-face sandwich, while my father, instead of the apple cider, had a beer.

In Germany, we had a different school system from that in the USA. Everybody had to start with grammar school at the age of six. At ten years of age, you either stayed for another four years in this school and then took an apprenticeship to become a hairdresser, salesgirl, carpenter, electrician, etc., or you changed over to the so-called "gymnasium," which was a high school, for eight more years. From there, you were able to go to college or attend a university. I took the test for the gymnasium. I prayed again very hard and got accepted. In grammar school, I had a very great teacher. I never ever forgot her. When I left this school, she took me aside and told me, "Ulla, now you leave us here for a better education. This enables you to have a good job later on in life. When you earn money, do not waste it on clothes or cosmetics. Spend it on yourself and travel, travel, travel. This will open your mind." I never forgot this, because I did and still do travel a lot.

Growing up, I was raised very strictly. My mother was the disciplinarian. She was the oldest of eight children and had always had to be a model for her siblings. I never heard the words "I love you." To show feelings was bad. Only weak people did that. It was important to use my brain and perform at school. When I came home with a C, I was yelled at; having a B, I heard "Why did you not bring home an A?" Should I bring home an A, nothing was said at all. So I did not care. One thing I found out at school. When I teased the teacher, I got accepted by my schoolmates. I concentrated on that and felt really good. We had very old teachers. They all would normally be retired. But all of the young teachers were killed or wounded in the war. Our English teacher was cross-eyed. She was very strict, and we all were afraid of her. We had six girls with the same name, "Ursula." Three were sitting behind each other, two on either side. She asked a question; we raised our hands to answer it. She pointed towards one, and all of us got up. She thought we wanted to tease her, but we were serious. She yelled at us, "You sit down!" All of us sat down. Since she was cross-eyed, it really appeared to all of us that she meant each of us. Our mathematics teacher had lost his wife and two children and his house during an air raid. He survived, but his back was very much hurt. He taught us not only math, but the meaning of life. In 1947, after the "Währungsreform," I still see him in front of our class. "Today we are all equal. We all have 48 Deutschmarks. There are no rich or poor people anymore," was his comment. The Reichsmark—our currency—was devalued and changed to Deutschmark.

Then we had "Fridolin." He was our Latin teacher. When he entered our classroom the first time, we all laughed, and he got this nickname, "Fridolin." He looked awful. He was very thin, ash-white in his face, and stuttered terribly. We later heard he just was released from a concentration camp. But we children didn't know this and teased him terribly. He never got respect, and after two years he was only allowed to teach religion, because we had learned nothing. I still feel guilty about this today—I too teased him a lot and felt good about it.

Once a year, the parents were invited to school to get to know their children's behavior and academics. Every year, my mother came back and was upset. What she heard from my teachers was, "Ulla would be able to be the best in class if she only would use her brain." That was unacceptable. My father was the opposite. He praised me and told me when I failed, "At least you tried." But my mother was more dominant. Through all this nagging, I became very shy and was not myself anymore. When I had to read out loud in class, my voice disappeared.

When we were sixteen years old, our whole class attended a "dance course," where you not only learned how to dance but good manners were taught too. Our whole class attended, as well as the boys of the boys' school, who were 17 years old. All my schoolmates were allowed to take this dancing lesson and were looking forward to it, except for me and two girls who were Mormons. My parents told me, "This is when all the dating starts, and you are too young for that." I cried my head off for weeks. In the end, they gave in. Now I had another problem. I still had pigtails and wanted to have a ponytail, which was fashionable in the fifties. Again, I had to cry till I got my wish. At the end of the dance course, which went over six months, we had "Schlussball," similar to the prom in the USA. My mother sewed me a gown, and then she found out that my decollete was too large, and she added a piece of fabric. I had a very nice dance partner. After the dance course, he invited me to a tennis match. But that was it. I never was allowed to see him again. I was not allowed to have a boyfriend, being only sixteen years old.

We lived in a town which had a population of eighty thousand—a small town. Everybody knew everybody, especially the upper- and middle-class people. My mother gave me the impression we were upper-middle-class. Later, I found out we were only middle-class people. My father was in sales for the largest brewery in those days. He had a very good salary. My mother used to be a bookkeeper before she got married. She looked down on all blue-color workers, or the laboring class. She looked down on our neighbors, who had their own painting business. I mentioned them before, because Margarete was my best friend. Even though they made a lot of money right after the war, I always heard, "They are nouveau riche and only blue color workers." I was told they had no manners. At first I did not get it, but it went into my belief system.

Today, I am wondering why my mother was like that, because her father was a blacksmith. I still remember my grandfather and my grandmother vividly. My grandfather had his own forge and three to four men to help him. They got housing and food from my grandparents. I saw my grandfather always in his blacksmith outfit. He was a stubborn, simple man, but he liked me a lot. I was the oldest grandchild. He taught me how to play cards. Quite often, I played with him, and he liked it. He still had a horse-drawn carriage and a horse. He took me on trips in his carriage after the war.

I learned from my parents that they were not allowed to get married because my father was Lutheran. When they were dating, my grandfather once spit in front of my father to show him that he was not worthy to marry my mother. After they were married, my father was his most beloved son-in-law. My grandmother was an angel. She came from a very good family. They were rich, and the children got a good education even in those days. She was not allowed to marry the blacksmith—my grandfather. But she did anyhow. She lived a life of her own through her religion. Every morning, she went to church. God was her source for bad and good. She was a very giving person, full of love. When I was a teenager I went to her quite often. She always listened to me and encouraged me to do good things.

My father's parents were totally different. His father came from a well-to-do family, and he was supposed to inherit the farm, the hotel and everything because he was the oldest son. He did not care about money or wealth. He left everything for his sisters, took only the money of his inheritance, and traveled. He wanted to see the world. He ended up in a big city, where he opened a café and bakery. There he found my grandmother, who thought she was someone very special because she went to the so-called "Toechterschule," the name for a girls' higher education institution in those days. Later it became the gymnasium. My grandfather was a very bashful man. He worked hard, was good-natured, and had a lot of humor. He loved nature and hiked a lot. My grandmother, on the other hand, attended the upper-class circle and met once a week with other ladies of her background. Grandfather teased her about this. And from my parents I learned this story. One day the ladies were having their afternoon meeting. They called it "Kaffeekraentzchen," or today we call it coffeeklatsch, where they have coffee and cake, but the main purpose of that meeting is to gossip about other people. In the middle of this meeting, my grandfather appeared and announced out loud, "Minna, we are bankrupt! We have no money left and have to cut all costs." It was a joke, and he wanted to embarrass my grandmother. She was. She was so upset.

My grandfather died when I was twelve years old, but my grandmother became ninety-two years old. At the end, she lived with my aunt. Every night she drank a little bottle of Champagne, a "piccolo." She was hiding it under her bed because she thought her little bottle would be stolen.

These were my grandparents—very normal, simple people— and yet, through my mother, I got a message to look down on other people. And I did. When I grew up, I never would have made friends with somebody who only attended grammar-school or did an apprenticeship.

I constantly heard about other people. Most of them were the town elite. How they thought and what they did was okay. I recall when I walked into town, I felt watched and criticized. I became so tied up that I almost stumbled over my own feet. When we visited my aunt, I heard my mother and her talking only about other people. They were gossiping and gossiping without end. One thing I got out of this. It must be great to belong to the upper class and be rich. They must have made it. Not only was my mother like that. All our friends and relatives behaved this way. I always was worried about what other people were thinking of me.

We still have a caste system in Germany. Through history there was an upper class and a lower class. The middle class was small. At the beginning of the twentieth century, we still had a monarchy. Emperor (Kaiser) Wilhelm II was in power from1888 to 1918. After World War I, Germany became a democracy, the so called "Weimar Republik." It did not last too long. In 1933, Reichs-President Hindenburgh nominated Hitler as his Reichschancellor, and from there on it got worse. Germany became a dictatorship. Again, people had to obey, but this time it was the party which was the leading society. But for hundreds of years, the monarchy was the leading caste, not only in Germany but all over Europe.

Even today there are royals around who have no important jobs and are not that rich anymore, but they think they are the top of society. My sister lives in an area where a lot of these royals live in little castles or big farms. She told me this: at one of those farms, a dentist had rented a stable which was converted into a living space or little house. One day, the baroness showed up with company. She opened the door of the dentist's living quarters and pointed out to her company, "This is how simple people are living." It happened in 1994.

After high school, I went to a business college in a big town, Dortmund. I commuted by train. This set me free. I bought a lipstick, and as soon as I left the train, I put it on. I put so much on that it must have looked awful. But I had to make up, because at home I learned that only "cheap girls" used a lipstick and make-up. In school, I got good grades. The teachers were young and treated us as adults. Here I found a little bit of my self-esteem. After this school, I was supposed to attend a university. All my friends went for a job, and so I too wanted to work. My girl-friend and I went job-hunting in this city. We were lucky and both found a job. We were on top of the world. But at home, I was in trouble. My father knew all the big shots of the large companies in my little town. He had connections. My parents were upset that I did not allow them to help me find a job. I was happy with the accomplishment I did for myself. I started as a secretary at BBC (Brown, Boveri, and Cie). I did not have to go through an apprenticeship because I had attended this business college. This was very important for me, because apprenticeship was for people of lower society. After a couple of days of working, I had had it. I went home and wanted to go back to school. My parents were firm. "You asked for it, you got it, and you stay" was their answer. So I worked there a couple of years. One of the first things I bought was a car. I always had longed for it when I was a little girl. In those days, women were hardly seen behind the steering wheel. Men were driving, and their wives were once in a while allowed to drive. Very few women owned a car. So I was very proud of myself.

On winter weekends, I liked to go skiing with my girlfriend. One weekend, we had a fight and did not talk to each other. I made up my mind and went by myself. It was the greatest weekend. It was a four-hour bus ride to the ski area from the city I lived in. On the bus were a lot of young people, but one young man looked like a movie star. All the girls were after him. After a bus ride of two hours, we stopped for a coffee break. Girls were all over him and trying to talk to him. I did not believe what happened. This young man was waiting for me and asked me to have something to eat with him. I was on cloud nine.

This was the beginning of our relationship. He worked in the same big city I worked in, and we saw each other every day and fell in love. I told him right in the beginning that sex for me is the same as murdering a human being. Only after marriage is sex allowed in order to have children. This was how I was brought up. I was commuting every day because I lived with my parents. I still had a curfew at twenty-two years old. It was ten p.m. Before I met Ernst-Walter, I was home around six p.m. Now I came home later, usually nine or ten p.m. My mother was outraged. She yelled at me every time. My friend told me that I had to cut the umbilical cord and do what I want to do. I listened to him and always waited for the last train which brought me home at eleven p. m. This was it. My mother called me "a whore." In our little town we had a movie club, and I became chairman of it. When we had meetings and I came home at eleven p.m., nothing was said. That was okay.

After dating for three years, we announced our engagement. My parents were totally against it. As much as my friend helped me to grow up and separate myself from my parents—which I needed—I started to doubt our relationship too. Once, he hit me when we were at a party. I was in shock. But after this, he was so nice and told me it was the alcohol and it would never happen again. In those days, I never heard about battered wives. His mother was running around quite often with a blue eye or swollen cheek. She always had an excuse. Today I know she was a battered wife, and I would have been too if I had married my friend. Whenever I had a doubt about our relationship, he talked me out of it. During our engagement, we were separated. He found a leading job in Munich, which was eight hundred kilometers away. Because of this, we saw each other seldom. After being engaged for two years, we planned our wedding. I still had doubts but always believed him. The wedding was set. I had my wedding dress. My religion teacher was willing to marry us in the chapel of an old castle close by my parents' home. Everything was set. One week before our wedding, I came home to my parents. In the meantime, I had another job. I lived two hours away by car and visited my parents only every other week. When I left that weekend, my mother mentioned, "There is still time to call off the wedding." Nothing more. This hit home.

When I came back to the village where I worked, I had to go to a party. My boss, who was a very big shot, was honored. There was dancing, and one of my colleagues wished me all the best for my married life, and I yelled out, "I am afraid." He looked at me like I had gone berserk. Next, I went to another colleague who was old and very much into philosophy. He once had offered to help me whenever I had a problem. When he heard my doubts, he told me to stop the wedding or I would be divorced soon. That was all I had to hear. I called my mother. She was delighted, telling me that she had prayed for it the whole night. She offered to cancel everything, and she did. To this day, I am very grateful for her actions.

Then I told my boss. My successor was already working for him. He was in shock. I threw everybody into shock, including myself.

Ernst Walter, my fiancé, had helped me to cut the string with my parents and listen to my own needs; but for a life together, we had not very much in common. I still was very immature, but about this decision I felt strong.

My boss told me to take off for two weeks and then come back. He wanted to fire my successor anyhow. I told him no way—I would never work for him. This woman could not suffer for my decision, and all employees and worker of the company—there were over 2000—would laugh at me. But my boss told me, "Only you and I are important. Nobody cares about the people gossiping. It will die down. I want you to stay with me. Take two weeks off, and then please come back." I took off and went home to my parents. My fiancé came two days later. He did not know anything. I told him, "I am not marrying you." He looked at me like I was making a joke. Then it hit him. He cried and begged me to stay with him and get married. But this time I was strong. I took off for two weeks and went into hiding. Before I did this, I told the director of human research to find me another job. Those weeks were terrible. After two weeks I went back to my company, and the director of human research had found me another good job. My boss did not give in to it. He told me he was letting that woman go anyhow. He could not work with her. "She can have that new job of yours." After that, I gave in and promised him, "I will stay with you forever and never get married." I should have kept my mouth shut.

After school, when I had my first job, I watched the secretary of the CEO. She had a ball. She got driven in a big Mercedes with a chauffeur. Her and her boss's offices were glamorous. I made up my mind to become a "Direktions-Secretary" (secretary of a CEO) like she was, and I did. I found this job at the "Stahlwerke Brueninghaus." My boss was the chief of three factories. The headquarters had over two thousand employees. This was where his and my offices were. Another factory had twelve hundred employees, and the third over eight hundred and ours over two thousand. When I started my job, my boss had me over in his office for a serious talk. He explained to me that we were very special and nobody of all the other employees was allowed to enter our offices. The only ones who were allowed were the executives, and they had to make an appointment with me. All calls coming in for my boss ended up at my phone line. I was not allowed to connect my boss with a secretary. I always had to connect to her boss and had to know what it was he wanted to talk about with my boss. I really was shocked. It was like he was God and wanted to be treated like that. I learned that this was not only the case in our company but in all huge companies in Germany. Again, when you were on top of those large companies, you looked down on other employees.

I liked this job very much. I got what I had dreamed of in my first job. I felt wanted and admired for the first time in my life. That had never happened before. We had a couple of limousines, and only executives were allowed to ask for one. I had to decide who got one and who did not. The drivers of these limousines washed my car when they were around. I did not even have to ask them. When my boss was away on business, his driver drove me in his big Mercedes to all the places I had to go. I really liked it. I got treated like I was someone special. That felt good. I did not like to type. When my boss dictated a letter, then I had to type it. I hated that, even though I was very fast at typing. Why did I only have to type what he thought? I had a brain too. I felt like a machine. It bothered me. I made up my mind that one of those days, I would be the one who dictated. Often, I let typists do my job when there was not secrecy involved.

Something else bothered me very much. Young people who started in our company and had only six years of the so-called "gymnasium," or high school, had to do an apprenticeship for three years. After this, they got a job in a department of the company. What I did not like was that the boys always got jobs as clerks, where they were able to climb up the ladder, and the girls became typists, where they were stuck or had to show a lot more effort to get out of this. Some girls were smarter than boys and yet had not the chance that boys had. I promised myself to do something about this.

I was told not to open my door to the public. When my boss was gone, I did open it and asked whoever went by to come in: typists, bookkeepers, and clerks. I loved people, and I chatted with them about their lives and families. Therefore, people liked me. My boss would have gone crazy if he had been around.

I was in this company when I broke off my engagement. I mentioned already how nice my boss was and how he stuck to me. I mentioned too that all the executives had to make an appointment with me to get to my boss or our boss. There was one nice guy. He was the youngest of all of them, only five years older than me, and not married. He was there when I broke off my engagement and saw all the turbulence I went through. When I was free, I realized he liked me very much, and we started dating. I forgot the promise I had made to my boss. When we went on a date, each of us drove for miles in his car so as not to be seen by people we knew. It was supposed to be a secret. It worked for a little while, till we ran into an apprentice. Our secret was out, and the rumor ran through the whole company. Shortly after that, we even ran into our boss. What did we do? We looked away. We felt like idiots. The next day, I went to my boss and told him that we were dating. He was not upset. He liked both of us very much. He only asked me to take it easy and to stay for at least another two years, because then the company had its four-hundred-year anniversary, and a big celebration was planned. Important people from government and industry were invited. I felt much honored by this. I promised to stay. I did. I really loved my job and became myself. I had a lot of responsibility and was the first lady of the company.

After one year of dating, Heinz and I became engaged and planned our wedding after one more year. I thought we would be married and then live happily ever after. We both read a lot of books together. One was by the French author Saint-Exupéry, *Un Sens á la Vie* (*Give Meaning to Your Life*). We had endless discussions about the future, our lives, and God. We had a great time. Heinz was a great skier, and he taught me the real way to ski in the Alps.

Heinz was Lutheran, and I was Catholic. This meant trouble. Heinz wanted me to become Lutheran. I was so confused and scared to change my religion. After my upbringing, this was a big sin. Well, after he realized this, he gave me three days to think it over. Becoming Lutheran….we marry or staying Catholic…. good bye. I went through a terrible three days. One thing I did not understand. He came from a background without religion, and he practiced the Lutheran faith only through friends. After three days of headaches, I told him that I loved him very much, but I could not change. His response was: "If it is that serious to you, let's get married." I was in shock that he took it that easy and made me go through three days of suffering.

I remember another time, when we first began dating, that I saw a different person in Heinz than what I had experienced as a colleague. We were talking about our future, and he told me that whenever he married, his wife would have to be honest, clever, reliable, loving, efficient, thrifty, a good cook, caring, etc., etc., .etc. Again, I was in shock and told him, "You know, you have to marry an angel, not me." These were two shocking situations during our dating.

Heinz came from a totally different background than me. His parents never pushed him into anything. They never told him what to do. They were uneducated, simple people. Out of four children, he was the oldest and the only one who attended the gymnasium (high school) and had made the "abitur" (graduation). He pushed himself to do this, and his dream—which he fulfilled—was to become an executive (prokurist) in a large company. During his school years, he worked as a blue-collar worker to earn money.

What a difference from me. I never was allowed to do this. I learned to look down on people like that. When I was ten years old, I had an idea. My girlfriend and I went into a public park and picked lots of flowers. We made little arrangements, went to the open market, and tried to sell them. In loud voices, we yelled: "Flowers for sale, only one deutschmark!" Nobody bought anything. So we reduced the price to half a deutschmark. After a while, a woman came towards me and asked me, "Aren't you the little Naaf (my maiden name)?" When I came home, my parents already knew what I had done. They yelled at me and asked me if I had no pride in me. They told me that I brought shame to my family. "We don't do things like that." In America, parents would have been proud of me and would have challenged my sales talent.

After being engaged for one year, we married. I started my marriage expecting Heinz to make me happy like all the fairy tales. They married and lived happily ever after. The fairy tales ended with this, but our marriage started. I lost myself and became Heinz's catering mate. I forgot myself. He never wanted this or asked for it, but I was raised this way. I still remember my mother always telling me that I would never be a good housewife. So I did everything for him but packing his suitcase or cleaning his shoes. Through Heinz's constant giving character, I learned not to be like that, rather to do something for myself and ask him to do things; but it took years.

Heinz wanted me to stop working. He made enough money. I did not need to work. I was very upset, because I loved my job. I debated with myself: "Do I fight it or give in?" Well, after a lot of thinking, I gave in. My thoughts were that when I had a baby, I would have to stop anyhow, and all the fighting would have been for nothing. And so it was. Our Kirsten was born exactly nine months and six days after our wedding. My parents liked Heinz very much. My mother visited us always when I told her on the phone that I was bored.

She had been working as a social worker since my sister and I had left home. She went to a lot of seminars and took care of children who came from broken homes. After I was married, she told me once that she had been too strict with me and that she was glad that I rebelled. This made me feel good. We had a great relationship now. I was the first-born and she had raised me the way she was raised as the first-born of eight. Therefore, she had been too strict.

Through my boss, we got a very nice apartment. The company owned apartments for blue-collar workers and apartments for executives. We got one of the better ones in a nice neighborhood. Now I was a housewife. At first, I enjoyed it. I slept in—what a luxury! I read a lot of books. I had to have a cleaning woman. There was not even enough to clean. But by our standards, one had to have one. That bothered me very much. I did not like having someone around the whole day. I liked my privacy. After a while, I became very bored. One more thing I realized: colleagues who used to be very friendly when I was working didn't look at me anymore. I felt low. I only was an extension of my husband. I did everything to show I was worth something. I cooked, which I liked. We had lots of fruit trees in our garden, so I canned apples, pears, plums. The company sent a gardener every week. There was nothing to do in the garden. I did not like that anyhow. But I sewed. Once, we had to go to a black-tie governmental function in Bonn (in those days the capital of Germany). Important people from politics, the economy, and the arts were invited. I sewed my own evening gown. I sewed not only this dress; no, I sewed a lot of dresses, curtains, everything. When the children were born, I sewed dresses for Kirsten, a coat for Ingo. I did a lot of knitting. When Ingo grew out of this coat, I enlarged it by knitting little pieces and adding them to the arms and length. Heinz got a sweater. I got a sweater. I wanted to show Heinz and the world that I was a good housewife. My mother's words, "You never will become a good housewife," were still haunting me.

I did get very busy after Kirsten and Ingo were born. I was happy and proud to be a mother. But I never had learned how to handle babies or little children. So when Kirsten was born, I overdid it. I kept her away from all kinds of germs. I made her really sick. I was afraid I would do something wrong and she would die. I did not put her in front of the television; the waves could do her harm. When Ingo came along, I stopped this behavior. I did not have time for this anymore, and he became a lot healthier. He was fast in everything. Once, I caught him drinking out of a puddle on the street. It was very hectic with two little children, and I was overdoing it. I was a nervous, neurotic mother. Everything had to be perfect: the children, the apartment. Heinz was the opposite. Through him, I tried to learn to relax. Every evening when he came home, he helped me. Either he took care of the children and put them to bed while I made dinner (the main meal we had at twelve a.m.) or the opposite. That felt very good.

I was not raised like this. I was raised to be a good housewife, mother, and spouse. During my childhood, my father was a male chauvinist. He had the final say in everything, and my mother catered to him. Every morning, she cleaned his shoes. To this day, I hate cleaning my shoes. My father always got served first by my mother at dinner. I never saw him doing chores around the house. He did not need to do it. He was the provider, and that was enough. I had a very sad experience. Two weeks before he died, he visited us. Coming home from a supermarket, I heard somebody playing the piano. I went downstairs to see who it was. It was my father. I had no idea that he was able to play the piano. I never had heard him. He never had mentioned it. I listened for a while. He did not see me and kept on playing. After ten minutes, he saw me and stopped right away. He was ashamed. I was so thrilled and took him in my arms and showed him my joy. He was seventy-four years old, and this man started to cry. I never saw him crying. I told him how proud I was of him and asked why he had never told me about his talent. He cried and said, "It's all over anyhow." Two weeks later, he died. It was the first time he had showed his feelings; he never was allowed to do so. Therefore, I thanked God that Heinz was no chauvinist.

I did not like the town we lived in. It was okay when I was working, because I always traveled around; but now, being married with two little children, I wanted to get out. Often Heinz took me along on a business trip and I brought the children to my parents.

They were happy. This way, I even was able to go on vacation with Heinz after Kirsten's birth. She was six months old when we vacationed in the Alps, and my parents took care of her. When I came back, she did not recognize me anymore. My mother was with me after Kirsten's birth and after Ingo's birth. She died when Ingo was only seven months old and Kirsten two years and five months. When she was buried, there were a lot of those children and teenagers whom she took care of. She must have touched their lives, which gave me a lot to think about.

Then my life changed drastically. My dream of getting out of that little village came through. One day when I was ironing, Heinz came home from an interview. He was offered a job in another, bigger town at one of Germany's largest stainless steel companies. He had a big smile on his face. "We can move to a big city."

"Where to?"

"Guess" was his answer.

I was thrilled. "Bonn, Berlin, Hamburg, Munich?"

"No" was his answer. "Further away."

"Paris, Rome, London?"

Again, "Further away."

I now screamed, "New York?"

"Yes!" I heard now.

I was overwhelmed with joy. New York...I had only thought in my dreams that I ever would go there. The job he was offered at this company was still occupied by a man who would retiree in three years. These three years we were offered to move to New York, and Heinz was supposed to build up the stainless steel business for this German company, "Edelstahlwerke Buderus," in the United States. We were supposed to have the office and an apartment in Manhattan. The children were two and four years old, just in time to start school in Germany after those three years when we were back. What an opportunity!

I was thrilled and started right away to tell everyone. Well, my father was very sad, but he encouraged us. I think I would have felt guilty to do this move if my mother had been alive. Actually, today I think she died for me, so that I was free to go. We told our friends and neighbors, yet there I got different reactions. One neighbor told me, "How can you take out your children of these surroundings and this good neighborhood into something unknown?"

This made me feel guilty. I went to a psychologist with my worries. "Are you happy to go?" was her question.

"Yes, yes, yes! I cannot wait to leave," was my answer.

She told me "Look, whenever you are happy, the children will be happy." But she recommended taking them out only ten to fifteen minutes in the beginning so that they would get used to the skyscrapers. I felt good again. I showed the children the squirrels when we went for a walk, because I thought this was the last time they would see these little animals. How wrong I was!

Now I had something to look forward to. Deep down in my heart, I was a gypsy. I always had felt that way. Some people were not able to understand me, and other people were thrilled with us for having this opportunity. We started to get ready, which meant we had to think about what to take along to the New World. Heinz went again and again on business trips to the States to find out what was what. What do we need to know? He talked to people from other German companies and found out that American people with families lived in the suburbs. Having children meant that it was important to move to a good suburb which had a good school system. Moving into an apartment in Manhattan would mean sending our children to private schools, which are very expensive.

Another thing he found out: Americans buy and sell their houses every time they have to move and make money by doing this. So he came back with the idea that we would buy a house and sell it after three years. This was shocking for me. In Germany, you save and save money and then build a house and stay in it forever. When you die, your children inherit it. I grew up in a house my grandparents had built and my mother had inherited. We were proud of this. But other countries have other customs. After another business trip, Heinz came back and told us "We have to live in New Jersey, Bergen County." He actually could rent an office over there from another German company, and it was supposed to be a good area to raise children. There went my dream of living in Manhattan, but what did I know? I still was able to get out of this little town we lived in, and it was supposed to be only thirty to forty-five minutes away from Manhattan.

Time went by fast. We had to think about what we would take along for three years. The company did move all our furniture and belongings, but some items we really did not need, like all the baby stuff, canning jars, some furniture, etc. They stored for us in Germany. One thing I did not want to take either were my baking forms, because in my opinion, no American housewife would bake herself. She would buy everything in the bakery. Our good Rosenthal china and our silverware we did not need. In my opinion, Americans never would entertain in an elegant way. They used a lot of plastic. I was so prejudiced. All this knowledge I had from magazines, newspapers, and television. At the end, I had the china and silverware packed. One day, two moving trucks pulled up in front of our house. One got loaded with all the stuff going to the USA, and the other one with all the stuff getting stored by the company Heinz worked for.

Time went by fast, and the moment of our move was here. Heinz had the idea to cross the Atlantic by ship. We never would have the opportunity to do this again, and the company would pay even for first class. I almost died. I was so afraid to get seasick. I wanted to fly, and Heinz bought plane tickets. My father told me, "You have to do what your husband wants to do. It is his job opportunity." Here I had it. I felt guilty. When Heinz told me he had the flight tickets, I told him, because now he could not change anything anymore, "After a lot of thinking, I would have gone on the ship with you." He was so thrilled and said, "I can change this," and he did. I was stuck, and the company bought tickets for the *New Amsterdam*, a Holland America Line ship which left from Rotterdam the Old Country. I went to a doctor and asked for a medication in case I became sea-sick.

The last week, we stayed in a hotel, and all the farewell parties started. This was very sad. We had to say goodbye to all our friends and relatives. On the day of our departure, the company sent a car with a driver to bring our family with twelve boxes, all our clothes, to Rotterdam. None of our relatives came along. The *New Amsterdam* was a beautiful ship. They still were fixing it up, painting the outside because it was crossing the Atlantic back and forth. I still recall the sad feelings when we pulled out of the harbor. A band was playing farewell music. When would I see good old Germany again? Where was I going? What would happen to us? Heinz and I were staying at the railing. Heinz was carrying Ingo, I had Kirsten, and he must have realized my thoughts. He put his arm around me. "Moglie (my nickname), as long as we four are together and stick together, nothing can go wrong." I cried anyhow.

Now our life on board started. Ten days we were supposed to be on board, with two stop-overs: one in Southampton, England,

and the other one in Le Cob, Ireland. We had two gorgeous cabins with a foyer for each and marble bathrooms. They were more like a suite than a cabin. The steward who was designated to our suites introduced himself. We decided Heinz would sleep with Ingo in one room and Kirsten and I in the other one. The ship was moving already when Ingo asked, "When do we go on board?" in his baby-language. We had to bring him to the window and show him the water.

Life on board was great. Every morning we got a schedule for the day. They had programs for the children and a nursery school. The restaurants were awesome. At our table, a lady from Ireland was seated. She was a registered nurse and worked six months in Ireland and six months in New York at a hospital. That was strange to me. I took my pills against seasickness, and we participated in everything. In the morning, we brought the children to the nursery school, where they met children who talked English—their future language.

One day, I picked them up and met another mother who was waiting for her two children. She told me that they had left Germany for good and were starting a new life in the USA. Her husband's brother was a butcher over there and had told them to emigrate to the New World. This was too much for me. How could someone leave Germany and go into something uncertain? This they did, with two small children. For me, this was inexcusable. There was no safety net for them, like health insurance or a well-known company like we had that took care of everything. Well…well…well. Today, I know better. Most Americans did this and left their birth country for a better living, for the American dream. This butcher must be a millionaire today. Later on, I bought all my sausage at German butcher shops like Schaller and Weber, Ehmer's, etc.

On the ship, we were surrounded by Americans. There were still two classes: first class and tourist class. We were in first class because the company paid for it. We never would have been able to do so and pay on our own. But the Americans around us paid on their own. Most of them were old, and some had a nurse. Quite a lot of them were wearing mink stoles. My dream always had been to get a mink coat, because in Germany all the *nouveaux riches* were wearing Persian coats, and I hated those. Mink coats were so expensive that we were not able to afford one. One Christmas, Heinz gave me a drawing with a mink coat divided into a lot of pieces and money for one little piece. He told me that piece by piece, I would get a mink coat. These Americans were wearing a lot of jewelry, even diamonds, and make-up. In Germany only the lower class was wearing a lot of make-up, and they were looked upon as cheap. The language got to us. In school, we had learned Oxford English, and their language was like having a banana in their mouths. "How can we stand this for three years?" I asked Heinz. Today, the English accent sounds different to me, because I am used to the American one.

We had such a good time. At night, when the children slept, we went over to the tourist-class dancing, because there were young people. One night, our steward came looking for us. "Your children are crying." We rushed back, and there they were, sitting together on one bed, arms around each other and crying non-stop. What kind of a mother was I? Leaving them alone, dancing, and having a good time!

We enjoyed life on board the *New Amsterdam* very much—so much that I did not take my pills against sea-sickness anymore. I became tired, and I did not like that. I wanted to participate in all the activities going on. One night, I was awakened by strange noises. Opening my eyes, I saw two guys in blue overalls. They were closing our windows with wooden plates and tightening them with bolts. I got scared and asked them what they were doing, how they came in. The answer was horrifying. "We are expecting a terrible storm." We were in the Irish Sea. Here I was. I had not taken my pills anymore. Shortly after they left, the ship started to rock, and it became worse. It made noises like it was falling apart. I thought to myself, "How can this happen?" The ship was built 1936 and now it was 1969. For thirty-three years it had been crossing the ocean. Why now? Kirsten was still fast asleep. I wanted to see how Heinz and Ingo were doing. So I walked over. When I opened my cabin door, there were two blue-collar workers sitting and robes were all over. Entering Heinz's room, I saw that he and Ingo were fast asleep. I got so scared. This was exactly what I had been afraid of. It got worse. We all got seasick but Heinz. He was the only one feeling okay. I was not even able anymore to change Ingo's diapers; Heinz had to do it. This horrible storm lasted three days. During these days, I did not see a dining room. Our steward did come a couple of times, offering some fruit. I was not able to look at it. The same happened with the children. Once, I tried to go up on deck. Someone had recommended this to me in Germany before we were leaving. We took the elevator up, and when I went outside, the angry water of the Atlantic Ocean was dancing in front of me. I felt worse. Immediately, I turned around and went back to my bed. For three days we had to go through this; then, all of a sudden, the ocean became calm and peaceful. Our ship was gliding smoothly through the waters. During the day, the sun even came out and surrounded us with her warmth. What a difference. We all awoke from our terrible sea-experience. The children were alive again, and we walked outside on deck, lay in the sun, and, when they were in

31

the nursery, Heinz and I took dancing lessons. What a change of life. All four of us got dressed up and enjoyed all the good meals in the dining room again. The food was very good.

Time went by fast with all the activities, and our last day on board was here. In the early morning, we approached the New World, our new home country for the next three years. We were so excited. We sailed under the Verrazano-Narrows Bridge. What a gigantic structure. It was connecting Brooklyn with Staten Island. We had to go upstairs on deck in order to really get the whole impression. All four of us were together, and far away we saw the Statue of Liberty. She came closer and closer. When we were in front of this beautiful lady, I was overwhelmed. She greeted us like so many before us with all her beauty. I had only seen her on photos, and here she was. The grandest Lady in the world majestically was welcoming us sea travelers…in her bronze dressing gown, with a candlestick in her hand. Since 1886, she had warmed the hearts of countless numbers of immigrants. Then we pulled into the Hudson River, and the skyline of Manhattan was right there. They still were building on one skyscraper which was supposed to become the tallest building in the world—the World Trade Center—but only one-third of the building was to be seen. I took photos and more photos. Then we anchored at the pier. Opposite of our ship was a parking lot where all the American friends and relatives were waiting for the passengers. We wanted to watch how Americans acted. There was a lot of waving and screaming. We did not expect anyone. We were strangers. But all of a sudden, someone was waving towards us. I did not believe it. It was Sigrid and her two children.

I had met Sigrid in Germany, in the hospital, when we each gave birth to our first child: her Michael and my Kirsten. We were eager to see our children grow, so we visited each other once in a while, always addressing each other with "Mrs." and the last name. In Germany, you only call your closest friends by their first name. Then we were pregnant again, and within four months, Sigrid's daughter Katrin and my Ingo were born. We visited each other quite often with our children. They became friends. After four years of knowing each other, her husband lost his job and he got an offer from a German company to work in New York. They packed up, and we said "Goodbye" forever. We became pen-pals. She wrote such interesting letters. They lived on the East Side in Manhattan, and she was the only mother on the playground. All the other children had nurses. She described how she let the children play in the elevator to keep them occupied and how she bred cockroaches by letting them eat all the crumbs in the toaster. She loved animals and did not know this kind till somebody told her. I always wrote her back that nothing interesting happened to me. A year and a half after they had left, I had great news for her. I wrote her that Heinz too had gotten a job in New York. Right away, a letter came back and she addressed me as "Ulla." She gave me my first lesson. In America, you always call your friends by their first names, and it would be terrible if we two Germans addressed each other as "Mrs." when all other Americans would call us by our first names.

And now here they were, Sigrid, Michael, and Katrin, waving towards us when our *New Amsterdam* anchored at the pier. What a joy. We felt a lot warmer in our hearts. It took a couple of hours till we were able to leave the ship, and then they only were able to see us for a little while because we got picked up by a businessman from the company that Heinz was renting his offices from. But the first thing Sigrid asked me was, "What kind of ship did you come over on?" Yes, our ship looked awful. The whole front was damaged.

What a difference from when we saw it in Rotterdam before we were leaving. I told Sigrid that we had a number eleven storm. In the meantime, I had learned that number twelve is the highest. I still recall when we went through customs, I got asked: "Where will you be living?" My answer was "Bergen County"—what did I know? The customs officer was impressed. "A nice area" was his answer. I was anxious to see this place.

Then we took off. The children and I were in the car of Heinz's business friend, and Heinz followed us in a rental car. My eyes became bigger and bigger when we drove through Manhattan, but I did not see too much. We took the West Side Highway and crossed the Washington Bridge onto Route 17. In the meantime, it had gotten dark, and I only saw lights on both sides of street. It did not end—light after light. I figured it must be one gasoline station after the other. I had to know and asked the business friend. He laughed, and I learned these were businesses: stores, offices...all commercial buildings. I did not know this from Germany. We did not have commercial buildings on the Autobahn. I had no idea then that this would become my shopping alley for the next years to come. After forty-five minutes, we arrived at the hotel, where the company had rented two rooms for us: one for the children and one for Heinz and myself.

I was in America. Our new life could start. It started right away. The next morning, we were sitting in the office of a realtor to buy a house. In Germany, we did not have realtors. You went to an architect and you built your dream house. Then you stayed in it forever. I grew up in a house my grandparents had built 1928. My mother had inherited it after my grandparents died. Through a statistic, I learned that 79 % of all Americans have their own house, compared to 28 % of Germans, but it is more expensive to build a house in Germany than in America.

I watched that realtor carefully. She was surprised that we just had moved a day before from the old country. She drove us around and showed us houses. This was very interesting, but strange. Day by day, we discovered the real-estate market. It was very interesting, and we got a glimpse of how Americans were living. After seeing forty-eight houses, we decided we would rather rent a house. We did not get a good interest rate for our mortgage, because we had no credit. Besides, people recommend us to rent in order to find out what was important. So we went to the King of Real Estate and took the first house we saw.

Heinz had to go to work, and here I was alone with the children in the hotel with two rooms. I was very eager to learn a lot about Americans. I watched television. One show interested me very much. It was with Barbara Walters, "Not for women only." I liked this, because I really got an insight into American thinking. How advanced and free. She pointed out all the problems we women have. I would have been to shy to talk about everything and stand up for my rights. I could not get enough from her. Therefore, I watched her every morning.

One day, I wanted to take a walk with the children to get fresh air. I left the hotel, and we went towards the next little town. All of a sudden, a car stopped, asking me if I need a ride. I thanked the driver and we went on. We did not see a single soul on the street walking like us. Again, another driver stopped, asking the same. I really got confused. Then a police car went by, stopped in front of us, and watched us a little while. Then, when we reached the car, the policemen asked us, very friendly, "Can I help you? Do you have a flat-tire?" Very fast, I learned that nobody is walking—everybody is driving. Kirsten, only four and three-fourths years old, discovered something too. "Mom, why are so many women driving a car?" It was true that in Germany, middle-class-people had only one car and men were driving them. That has changed rapidly today, but this was 1969.

Another day, I had had it and was bored, always sitting in this hotel with two small children. Heinz had to leave for a business trip. He flew out of La Guardia Airport. Since we had only this one rental car and he had to be at the airport very early, we decided that he would me from the airport, and the children and I would pick up the car. This gave us something to do. We were in a hotel in New Jersey. I learned that I had to go by bus into Manhattan and then by another bus to the airport. Our hotel was on Route 17 in New Jersey, where all the busses went by into Manhattan. The concierge told me to stay on the street and flag down a Short Line bus and then it would stop. All busses were going to Manhattan into Port Authority, where I could catch the other bus. I followed her advice.

Here I was, standing at the highway with two little children, flagging down bus after bus, and not one bus would stop. I was patient; this was another country. After a while, a man came towards us, asking, "What are you trying to do?" Well, I told him what I had in mind. He looked at me like I had come from another world. I can still hear his words today: "You are standing here by the highway with two little children in the rain, and it is cold. Most of the busses are express busses. Let me bring you to Ridgewood, to a real bus stop with a rooftop." I did not know what he was talking about, but I accepted his offer. He really was very friendly, and what could happen with two little children? On the way to Ridgewood, he asked me, "Where are you from?" When I explained I was from

Germany, he told me very happily that he was Dutch. I thought he too had only been in this country for a couple of days. "When did you come over?" was my question. Then I got confused. "Oh—I did not come over. My grandparents came over from Holland." I did not get it. How could he be Dutch when his grandparents immigrated into the USA? For me, he was American. Well, well, well. He brought us to the bus station, and we caught our bus.

On the bus to the airport, I experienced another eye-opener. The bus was filled. Next to me sat a businessman. When he saw my two little children, he started to talk to them. Ingo was always a very active little guy. He took him on his lap and gave him a piece of paper and a pen to keep him busy. I was in shock. This would never happen in Germany. There I was in charge of my children and had to keep them quiet. What a relief it was for me. I learned how much Americans like children.

When we found the car, we had to go on all the highways surrounding Manhattan and over two bridges, the Triborough Bridge and the George Washington Bridge. I had never been there, so I had looked up the map and pinned a little note on my dashboard. I drove like a German—very fast and always on the left side to pass by all cars. All of a sudden, being on the left side, the children were fighting, I saw my exit. How was I able to manage to get over to the right side? There were four lanes. With my blinker, I gave a sign, and, looking into the back mirror, I was in shock. Cars slowed down and gave me a sign to pull over. What a nice country! People were so polite. I made it home safe, had a car, and was able to explore more. I had learned a lot already just by picking up a car from the airport.

The next desire I had was to drive into Manhattan and discover this. I still was sad that we had not moved into this part of New

York, but now I was able to drive into it. This I did. One morning after we had dropped off Heinz in Hackensack, where he found a nice office, the children and I kept driving on into Manhattan. We had only been in this country a couple of days. I parked the car on yellow lines around Thirty-Fourth Street and took the subway, ending up at Battery Park. I had no idea about the system. Today, I would say it must have been the E-train or Train One, but I still don't know what I did. We were thrilled when we saw the Statue of Liberty again. We walked around, and my heart was filled with joy. We walked back to the subway and took a train uptown. Our guardian angel must have been with us, because we ended up where we took off. Our car was still there. Later, I learned that it was forbidden to park on those yellow stripes. I was lucky. We made it safely back to the hotel without a fine. Later, I also learned there were a lot of trains going uptown and downtown.

A couple of days later, I had another encounter with Manhattan. I was so anxious to explore this city. Sigrid, my only friend in this country, called from Westchester, where they had moved. She wanted to show me Manhattan in the evening, when our husbands were home and were able to watch the children. We were free. On the phone, she explained where I had to go and where I was able to park on the street after seven p.m.

In the meantime, our Volkswagen had arrived from Germany. It still had a custom license plate. We bought it in Germany and had shipped it over because we learned we could sell it easily in the USA and make money on it.

Now I took it into the city and parked it on the corner of Third Avenue and Forty-Ninth Street. There was a green awning at the house where I had parked. I looked at the sign and, yes, I was allowed to park there. Then we met at Rockefeller Center. I was overwhelmed by how beautiful the whole area was. Sigrid wanted to introduce me to a special American drink, the "whiskey sour." "I don't like whiskey," I told her.

"Oh, you have to try this—you will like it!" So she brought me to the Pan Am Building. In those days, there was a bar on the top floor overlooking Manhattan. What a place. The first time I saw Manhattan by night. These lights were enormous. Yes, and she was right—I liked her recommended "whiskey sour" very much. We had such a good time, and time went by very fast. Suddenly, we realized it was almost ten p.m., and we decided to go home. She wanted to bring me to my car, because she had parked in another area, but I had written down my corner: Third Avenue and Forty-Ninth Street. So off we went. I was in for a big surprise and adventure.

When came to my corner, there was another Volkswagen, and a man was still sitting at the steering wheel. I told him that I had parked my Volkswagen there. He was very friendly. "Well, I have been sitting here for thirty minutes and did not see your car."

I panicked. "What can have happened to it?"

"Oh," was his answer, "maybe it got towed away, or it is stolen."

Here I was, all by myself in this unknown city with no car. I went to look for a policeman and found one around the corner. He took me to the next police station. There I got asked a lot of questions and had to fill out forms. The policeman left. They asked me about my license plate number. I did not know it. I only knew it was a custom plate. They asked me about the registration papers. When they heard everything was in the glove compartment, they shook their heads. All of a sudden, after maybe thirty minutes, my policeman came back with a big smile. "Lady, I found your car." I was thrilled. He walked me to my car, and I was ashamed. Yes, I had parked at the corner I told him about, but opposite of Forty-Ninth Street, and that house had an awning too. He wished me a safe trip home and followed me in his police car up to the West Side so that I did not get lost again. I was so thrilled. God—New Yorkers really were friendly.

Next to us in our hotel was another family with children. Kirsten and Ingo were playing with them outside when Kirsten came running in to tell me, "Ingo is hitting those boys because they are talking so funny." He did not know it was another language than what he had learned.

We wanted to get involved, find a nursery school for the children so that they would learn English, find a women's club for me. Heinz was told at the office that you did this through your church. So, one Sunday afternoon, we went to the Catholic Church. After mass, we introduced ourselves to the pastor and told him our desire. He was very helpful, giving us the name of a nursery school and promising us to let the president of the "Rosary Club" know. He gave her our address.

The next day, a lady called and introduced herself as president of the Rosary Club and made an appointment to see me. It was Mary Frances. A couple of hours later, a German girl called me. It was Waltraud. Mary Frances had asked her to come along to meet this emigrant woman who was not able to speak English and translate for her. Waltraud and I were on the phone for an hour and found out that she did not have to translate because I did speak English. We found out we were the same age and had a lot in common. Waltraud explained to me not to be in shock when Mary Frances would come and kiss me. This is a custom in America. Wow! Now I learned another thing. Every night when I watched the Johnny Carson show, people kissing each other, I thought they were having an affair. This way I learned something. In Germany, you shake hands. I learned Mary Frances had seven children. Wow! In Germany, having two children was the most. She actually had two more later.

Then we met. Waltraud was right. Mary Frances came and kissed me hugged me like we had been friends for a long time. She was very sweet and full of love. Right away, she told me that she had seven children and showed me a photo of them: six girls and one boy. They all were dressed up, and the girls were wearing hats. It was a photo they had taken on Easter. I was impressed, but she was not wearing a wedding band, and this with all those children? I saw on her left hand something glittering. It must have been a zirconia ring—a make-believe diamond. I had learned in Germany that Americans wear and have fake stuff. This must have been it. We wear a golden wedding band on the left hand when we get engaged, and it gets moved onto the right hand when we get married. Later, I learned the truth: that all Americans got these beautiful diamonds, and they were genuine. Then I wanted one too. Later on, I learned from my American friends how they were astonished at me only wearing this cheap gold band and no diamond. This was another culture shock. Back to Mary Frances' visit: *yes,* I joined the Rosary Society.

Waltraud became my friend, and I was able to ask her all the questions I had, and she filled me in about American life. After we had moved into our rented house, I asked her where I could find a maid. She looked at me and said: "Look around, and you will see that American women clean their houses by themselves. They only take a maid when the house is too big and they really need one, and not to show off. Most German immigrants are maids." This set me free. I always had so much energy and did not need one.

This country was interesting, and I wanted to learn as much about it as I was able to. The media and books in Germany had given me a wrong idea. So much was different from what I thought it was. Heinz and I made up our mind not to go back to Germany during these three years, but to explore the country and its people, and that we did. I had more time to do it than Heinz, because he had to work.

One thing got my attention already. Television and the magazines were different than in Germany. They catered to all people, from the rich to the poor. If there was a survey on the streets, they interviewed people we Germans never would have talked to, but we would have an opinion about them—that they were rednecks or looked stupid. They must look sophisticated and smart to be interviewed. We always had an opinion about everyone. Then there were the magazines. My hobby was cooking, so I always read the recipes. In Germany, the recipes often called for ingredients I never heard of, and everything was very expensive. They were more for the rich people who were able to afford all the ingredients. Here, they were for everyone; even I was able to afford everything. When I read an article in Germany, they were people to look up to, and here they were about the "little people" (Leona Helmsley's expression) too Sometimes, I read magazines from both countries, and right away I realized by the content, "Oh, this is from the US" or "Oh, this is from Germany." It was very interesting, but I felt good about it. I realized this is the country by the people, of the people, for the people. All people count.

After six weeks, we moved into our rented house. We had to wait for our furniture to be shipped over. It was a small house with only two bedrooms and one bath, but we were moving back to Germany after three years; so what?

The moving truck was still outside when a neighbor came over. She was thrilled that Germans were moving in next to her, because she was German. Again I asked, "When did you come over?"

"Oh, no, my mother and father came over when they were young." She had grown up in Queens, where her parents had worked their way up to open up a deli. Here I was again; yes, I had heard that before. She saw that we did not have a lamp. All electrical items we had left in Germany, because the currency was different. We had 220 voltage, compared to 110 over here. She left and came back with a lamp. Then she realized there was no television. We had enough to do and did not need this, but after a couple of minutes she was there with a television. Another neighbor came over. It was Gloria. She was Italian, but I did not ask anymore when she came over from the old country. Actually, she was raised in Brooklyn, and again, her parents were emigrants.

When I was growing up, I never heard of anybody being proud to emigrate to the US or Australia; only the very poor people did it, and they were looked down upon. We had relatives who had done this two generations ago, and they were still marked as "runaways." Only some people had left Germany around 1950, being afraid of another world war. I got a totally different opinion. I started to look up to all the immigrants, who had suffered so much to have a better life. They did not come over on a luxurious ocean-liner like us, but under most terrible circumstances. In school, we had learned about the Pilgrims on the "Mayflower." Now I started to understand what those people went through, and even why the Americans still were proud of their ancestors. Therefore, the spirit to help others was still around, and therefore families are still sticking together. This was a revelation for me.

Everybody called us "Heinz" or "Ulla" right away. In Germany, we would have been addressed as Mr. or Mrs. Reichhardt. This gave me a warm feeling, like I was wanted. I learned they all treated us with warmth, like their ancestors coming into this country wanted to be treated when they "stepped just off that boat." Well, I always thought I was a jetsetter, but I liked this gesture a lot more.

Mary Frances, whom I had met before, invited me with the children one day for lunch. Heinz had to work. Now I met her seven children. It was a lovely lunch. I had fed my children before, because in Germany, children were to be unseen. What a surprise. She was upset. "Here in this country, children are precious, and we adore them," she taught me. I never did this again. Her children performed an Irish step dance for us. She always listened to each child when one came with a question. What another eye-opener for me. I liked this.

I learned American eating habits through Gloria. In Germany, people thought of American women as not being able to cook— only open cans and do it the easy way. I was very prejudiced and thought the same. In Germany, we have our big dinner around lunchtime, coffee and cake around four in the afternoon, and then only something light at night. Gloria invited us for dinner when Heinz was on a business trip. I did not expect too much. First I was offered a drink and hors d'oeuvres in the living room—that was different. Then we were asked over to the dining room. The table was set very nicely. Gloria served spaghetti Bolognese. It was delectable. I finished the whole plate. As a German with good manners, you never leave anything on the plate, and I was hungry. Then I did not believe it: she served the entrée with meat, vegetables, and pasta. This was too much but I did not want to insult her. Again I finished the plate. I was stuffed. There was another surprise: coffee and cake as dessert. I ate it, but I felt really sick. Gloria, as an Italian, was the greatest and sweetest hostess. She always offered and offered her food again. "Mangia," a sign of love! Why was I so arrogant as to think "Americans don't cook"? The media had given us Germans such wrong information. Actually, this was more than what we did in Germany when we had people over for dinner.

Another thing I learned. Dessert always is coffee and cake. That too was different. Like I wrote before, we have this in the afternoon, between meals, and I always bought cake in Germany to show people I had money enough to buy it. Therefore, I always asked my American friends, to make them feel good, "Where did you buy it?"

The answer was "Oh, no, I baked it." Ignorant or arrogant as I was, I had stored all my baking tins in Germany because I never expected Americans to bake. Now I had to go out and buy new baking tins.

I realized what a big mistake I had made when Mary Frances came over the first time to invite me to the Rosary Society. It was around five p.m., and I offered her coffee and cake. She looked at me, very upset, and asked: "Do you have a drink?" We had bought six bottles of alcohol on the ship when we came into this country, because they were duty-free. I told her what we had and she asked for a scotch. Yes, she was Irish. Instead of coffee and cake, Americans have a drink in the late afternoon. They have happy hour.

I really got to like my neighbors and got very busy. Only eight weeks after we moved in, we had a New Year's Eve party.

I joined the Rosary Club and the Welcome Wagon Club. American women amazed me. They were so active. It was amazing how they put all their energy into good sources, like making money for charities. "Money" for me was a dirty word. You have it and don't talk about it. But here, everybody talked about it. This was capitalism in its best form. I always understood capitalism as people are going only after money and not having any feelings or inner meaning. Was I wrong! What another eye-opener again. American women not only were very active, giving their time and energy to good sources, but they were more themselves.

I remember one meeting when the president—it was Evelyn—was in front of all the members giving a speech, and her baby cried. She took him in her arms and kept on talking. This was very impressive and totally different from my German upbringing. Evelyn and I became friends and still are friends today.

Summer came fast, and I loved the ocean. A couple of times we had been to Jones Beach—what a marvelous place! My neighbors told me about a club where they went. Ten minutes away, there was a lake with sandy beaches, all kinds of activities for the children, a clubhouse, and a nice wooded area with picnic tables and benches. You had to pay to be a club member. I liked the ocean so much, but they talked me out of it. They were right. We became members of Brookside and enjoyed it very much.

Before I went the first time, Waltraud called me. She asked me what kind of bathing suit I had. When I told her it was a bikini, she informed me that it was impossible to wear that. So I had to buy a one-piece suit, and she was right. Everybody was wearing this; some even had a little skirt around the suit. During the week, early in the morning, I went with the children and stayed till suppertime. All our new friends were there. One day, my German friend Sigrid came with her two children to join us. Sigrid and I were talking when we heard over the loudspeaker: "The mothers of the two stripping girls are called." We looked at each other and realized this could only be our daughters. Yes, they were exchanging bathing suits in the open and thinking nothing about it, because they were raised with the idea that nudity is nothing bad. When we became more "free" in Germany, I always thought this trend came from the USA, but again I was wrong.

There was a German butcher in the neighborhood where I was able to buy German magazines. I had them lying around one day when my neighbor came over. She was shocked to see those magazines and asked me if they were "Playboy magazines." No, they were family magazines, but those cover girls were wearing string bikinis, and nobody thought anything about it in Germany; but here, people were more puritan.

Most of the people had always the same question: "How do you like America?" They were expecting my answer to be, "It is the greatest country in the world." I was not ready for that. I loved Germany and felt like a German. In whatever country you get raised, you get used to the way of life, and you love it. It takes a while to adapt another culture. I thought Americans were arrogant to expect me to like their country. Well, later on, I changed my opinion.

I discovered one great thing. Mink was quite a lot cheaper than in Germany. Heinz kept his promise, and one Christmas, I did not get money for a piece of mink, but a whole full-length mink coat. I felt like a queen and wanted to show off with it. My neighbor Helen was happy for me; her remark was, "Wear it in good health." I got more of this from other people. Nobody envied me like they would have done in Germany. This was a capitalistic country. I thought these things were important. But I learned things are not important at all; people are important—the *Mensch*. It took me awhile to really appreciate this, because I grew up in totally different surroundings, but I liked this.

It was amazing to me how fast the children learned English, or better, American. Ingo still spoke baby language, but Kirsten was able to speak American after six weeks without an accent. Both went to nursery school, and at home I let them watch *Sesame Street*. We had to struggle for years to learn a foreign language in school, and here they did it so fast.

Being raised Catholic, I was sad that in Germany, very few people went to church, and the saying was: only the old and stupid ones are going. I still felt it was a sin to miss mass on a Sunday, and always went with the children. It was a relief, coming into this country where almost everybody went to church and there were so many different denominations. It did not matter which religion you belonged to, but that you belonged to one. Nobody judged the other one for doing so. I felt at home, because most of the people around me were Catholic, of Irish or Italian descent.

During the years, I got very busy. My calendar was always occupied. They asked me to be a chairman of this and that in those clubs. How was I able to do something like that with my background? Being a perfectionist, I felt I should be better prepared in everything before taking on this responsibility. At first, I only agreed to be in charge of making the coffee and having people bring cakes for the break when we had meetings of the Welcome Wagon Club; but more and more, I accepted all offered jobs. I was not able to say "No." My calendar was always full. It made me feel good.

I invited our new friends to dinner-parties. I was not used to dinner-parties and will never forget how nervous I was when I gave the first one, with hors d'oeuvres, drinks, appetizer, entrée, and dessert—what Gloria hat taught me. It was work. Heinz helped afterwards to clean up.

We loved our life in America. Often we drove into Manhattan, which really offered the best of the best. If Heinz did not come along, I went with girl-friends. We explored the museums, the opera, musicals on Broadway, great restaurants. I fell more and more in love with Manhattan. Where in the world did you get offered what this city offered you? I loved art and had many art books. I will never forget when I went the first time to the Metropolitan Museum of Art and saw the real paintings I only knew from my books. I got goose bumps. Or another time, we went to the Metropolitan Opera, and here we heard Maria Callas. I never, ever would have been able to hear her in Germany. I felt as if I were in heaven.

More and more, we fell in love with America and made up our minds not to go back to Germany. Three years went by so fast, and we were so busy. We had made many friends and felt more and more at home. I never got homesick, because I felt wanted. We loved the country and its people and had grown into the American way of life.

What helped even more in making the decision not to go back to Germany was the fact that Heinz' German company wanted us to live in a certain area upon our return. We were supposed to live where all the executives were living because Heinz had earned this great job—in good English, we had to show off. We had to do again what society wanted us to do. In the meantime, we had learned in America to do what we wanted to do. Even though Heinz would have had that job where we would have been members of the upper class and had all the material things, we had learned that things are not as important as human beings. To stay in the US was the biggest decision we ever made in our life, and we never regretted it.

We had to settle for good now. Again, we went to a realtor to buy a house—our house. We found a great one. After three years, the children and I went to Germany for the first time to let the company know what to ship over from all the stored boxes. They were very kind and sold for us what we did not want and shipped over the rest. My father was heartbroken. He had waited for us to come back, because he was alone. My mother had died before we went to the US. I think if she had been alive, I never would have moved to the US. I would have felt guilty for going away and taking away her grandchildren.

After we moved into our house, we experienced the same friendliness of the Americans again. Our neighbors were great. We had block parties and dinner parties, and everybody was there to help. I had so much free time. Heinz was gone the whole day, and the children started school! With a girlfriend, I often went into the city, which means Manhattan. We explored each part of it with all its offerings. Again, I joined what was now called the Newcomers Club and said "Yes" when they offered me a job. I was chairman of the "Gadabouts," which meant that once a month we took a trip, and I had to arrange it. I joined the book club, where we read a book and discussed it, and so much more. What I liked most was to meet people and to learn about their lives. Since I was a parent, the school asked for participation too, this was great. I was asked to be a Brownie leader when Kirsten joined the Girl Scouts. I said no—how was I able to do this? I never was a Girl Scout, and I did not know any songs and so forth. My upbringing was German. But they had a way of talking me into it. They sent me to a seminar where I learned about it, and then I was sworn in and became a Girl Scout. I became a Brownie leader. When Ingo became a Boy Scout, I was his den mother. Yeah, I was busy, but I liked it. I learned so much.

The children were busy too. There were so many after-school activities: Boy Scouts, Girl Scouts (as I mentioned before), baseball, soccer, softball, ballet, and piano lessons for Kirsten, trumpet lessons for Ingo, etc., etc.

I never knew anything about baseball and football. One day I was sitting on the bench when Ingo had a baseball game, and a woman came asking me, "What inning is it?" I did not know what she was talking about. What should I tell her? "Hum, hum I just came too, and I haven't found out yet," I replied. I always applauded when the parents of Ingo's team applauded. This way I was on the sure side.

On one Memorial Day, Kirsten and I had to march in the parade. I was in full uniform as her Brownie leader. Our whole troop was marching. We had to lay down a wreath at the park to honor all the soldiers who had died in World War II. I got a weary feeling. Here I was marching as a German girl. These used to be our enemies. They had killed my two uncles. For the first time in my life, I realized how terrible wars are. People had to suffer, and people did not hate each other. People were people all over the world and wanted to live in peace. Actually, our friend Paul had served in World War II. He and Heinz were best friends today. Had they been in a war, they would have been out to kill each other. I became an anti-war believer.

The American people amazed me. Everybody was so friendly and polite. There was no shuffling; everybody stood in line. Everybody talked to everybody. I could talk to strangers, or strangers sometimes gave me a compliment. I was not used to that. You very seldom got a compliment in Germany, and when you got one, you turned it down by saying "Oh, that's old," "Oh, that is terrible," or "I have had it for a long time." Over here, you enjoyed it and said "Thank you." When I walked in the morning, every person said "Hallo" or "Hi." Sure, they were strangers, but friendly. After a couple of years, being back in Germany, I tried this too. It did not work. The person stopped walking and looked at me like I had come from another planet. I liked the friendliness in America. It made me feel good and the other person too.

What amazed me more was people did not judge each other. This gave me a free feeling, knowing whatever I did; my friends and neighbors did not judge me or talk about me. It gave me the freedom to do whatever I wanted to do. I still was very German and found myself judging people. When friends only said nice things about other friends, I thought to myself, "They are phony." I knew all the bad habits and bad stuff about them, so why bother to tell nice things? Later, I learned how great it is to think and see only the goodness in people. I wanted to be treated like this.

I will never forget how we were at a party at one neighbor's house, and I saw fingerprints on the oven. I judged her to myself: "How dirty she must be. Why didn't she clean before the guests arrived?" Or another time, another neighbor had dirty steps going into her house. I looked down on her. Another neighbor told me once, "I have to wash my kitchen floor today. I have not done it for four weeks." I was in shock. Every week, I washed all my floors, vacuumed the carpets, etc.—cleaned, cleaned, cleaned as I had learned it! I washed the windows every week, certainly every other week. From my friends, I learned they washed them once a year. When I come into a house of a German friend today, I realize they still clean as they had learned to do. At a lunch recently, one of my German friends mentioned how dirty the grout in the kitchen of her American daughter-in-law was. Coming home, I looked at my grout and started to clean. After all these years, my German upbringing came back. I forced myself more and more to overlook dirt—or better said, to overlook unimportant things. Heinz was great; he even helped me by talking me into it. With the years, I changed, but it took me a long time. I forced myself not to make our bed first thing in the morning, let it go, and do something nice for myself. Heinz gave me a compliment, and this country with its people helped me too. Today I only clean when I have to and concentrate on more important things. I would rather read a book. If I had done this earlier, I would have had a lot more time to spend with my children, like my girlfriend Mary Frances. In the meantime, she had nine children. She always had time for each child. The house was a mess. But when they were grown up, each child became a happy adult.

I realized the pioneer spirit was still around. People were helping other people. Charity was a big deal. If you had made it in this country, you gave back to the poor, the sick, or the needy. People volunteered for all different occasions.

You never look down on people with a lower job, I learned, too. Whatever you do is okay as long as you have a job. You don't get judged. I used to look down on a salesgirl, a maid, or hairdresser. In this country, each job got appreciated as long as you worked at all. Nobody ever was looked upon by the job she or he did. I realized that people therefore were a lot happier in their jobs and more creative. Whatever they did, they liked it. Even when there was a poll about an opinion on television, dumb and intelligent people got asked about their opinion. Not in Germany. All people got treated as people and were accepted for what they are, not what they are supposed to be. How did the constitution start? *We the people*... That was great.

Slowly, I learned what freedom means. I was able to be me. Nobody judged me or my doings, nobody put me down, and nobody expected something from me. One day, when Heinz had gone to work and the children were at school, I asked myself: "Why am I not happy?" Here I was, surrounded by a healthy environment, a great husband, and wonderful children. I had what every woman needed. Yet I still desired furs and diamonds, thinking that make me happy. Heinz was so sweet. Yes, he bought those things for me. But they didn't do the trick either. I was a nervous, always-running-around young woman who did what everybody told her to do. I yelled at my children and realized I did the same thing my mother had done to me. Like mother, like daughter. I yelled when they spilled something, they still tell me today. I called them names. I wanted to form them into my belief system without letting them be themselves. When I saw genes they had inherited from me that I did not like, I scolded them for it their behavior. Kirsten was a lot like me, and, poor girl, I did not accept her for this. I did not appreciate her, because I did not like myself. Kirsten was never afraid, and she rebelled as a teenager like I used to do. I did not understand it till one day when I was sitting at an opera in Chicago. I do not know anymore what I saw, but it hit me. I was not giving Kirsten unconditional love. I did not accept her for what she was. From that day on, I changed. I never forgot to say three little words after talking to both of them—"I love you." But what struck me was that I said it in English, even though we always spoke German. I had not learned those words in Germany, but in America.

I had never learned to be myself. I always was a daughter, wife, mother, or employee, doing what I was supposed to do, what everybody told me to do. Yes, I did all of this because, as I learned later, I was a perfectionist. I will never forget the day when Mary

Frances came by and told me, "We have to love ourselves." She had been to a seminar and had learned this. It was a shocker for me. Till now I had loved everybody but me. It was very selfish to do so. But was that why I was not happy? I started to read books. They called them "self-help books." The first one was by Dr. Joseph Murphy, *The Power of Your Subconscious Mind.*

Heinz was a wonderful husband. He let me be myself and never told me what to do. I will never forget how, when we still lived in Germany, he brought asparagus home from a business trip to Holland. Asparagus was a delicacy and very expensive in those days. I burned it. He was not upset. "You tried hard" was his response. When he traveled, he packed his own suitcase. In the neighborhood was a woman whose husband traveled a lot too. One day she told me he yelled at her for packing the wrong stuff. Was I happy not to be someone like her! He supported me too by telling me that I am an optimist. I did not know that. He was not a workaholic like most men are. Even though he was Vice President of a large German company, he came home every night at six p.m. Sure, sometimes there were exceptions, but this was not the rule. He called me when he left the office, and dinner was ready when he walked in. Family for him was number one. I thought I was blessed. Some friends of ours think they are irreplaceable at work. They are workaholics.

Most of my girlfriends went back to school when our children were in their teens. I wanted to do the same. What I was really interested in was law. This was something I wanted to go back for and then later on help women who were in trouble or any other underdogs. From my father, I had inherited a sense of fairness for everyone; therefore, I liked law. Heinz was against it, and how. I did not know why, because he was always so giving and understanding of everything I did. Normally he was not like this. He gave me so much freedom. Even one American girlfriend once told me, "He is like an American husband, not a German," which was true but now? I asked myself, "Do I fight it and go for it, or do I give in?" Well, I gave in, as I was taught to.

Another thing I did: I took a travel agent course at a close-by school. I did it for fun. "Maybe one of those days I will open a travel agency; who knows?" But then a couple of years later, I was surprised. Heinz came home from work with an advertisement from the Wall Street Journal, where an agency was looking for a German-speaking tour guide. He asked me: "Isn't this something for you?" Oh, yes, it was. I had always liked people, liked traveling. With my German girlfriend, I went into the city and applied for this job. We got accepted but were told we had to participate in seminars and get trained for it. Both of us were on cloud nine. We both felt wanted in a country where we were not raised or educated, where we were strangers. This really made us feel so good. We became one of the workforce. A sad thing happened. My girlfriend was not allowed to go for it. Her husband—yes, he was German—told her she did not need to work. He too was a Vice President of a large German company. I was glad to have Heinz, who was very generous. I went to seminars and took the license test for New York City, which meant I had to learn the whole Michelin Guidebook about New York.

I was thrown into my new job. Quite a lot of Germans were coming. It was a big business. I had to study a lot, but I liked it. I learned so much about my new country, about her history, about fauna and flora. The Germans wanted to know everything, and they were prepared very well. They had read all kind of tourist books before coming over. I always had loved New York, or better,

Manhattan. Now I had to give city tours and sell this city. I did it with such an effort that I often heard, "We can feel your love for this city; actually, you transfer that love to us." I started to take jobs on weekends, when Heinz was home for the children. He offered to do this. I stayed with my people in a hotel in Manhattan.

The first tours I did were like this: On a Thursday, a group of people flew into Kennedy Airport, where I picked them up. On Friday morning, I gave them a city tour. On Friday afternoon, we took the Circle Line around Manhattan. On Friday evening, we had dinner in a nice restaurant and then saw a musical on Broadway. On Saturday morning, we flew to Niagara Falls, where I had to show them everything, coming back late in the evening. On Sunday morning, we went to Washington, DC, by bus. We had a city tour and lunch in a nice restaurant at the Potomac River. Again, we came back to the hotel late at night. On Monday morning, I had to give them a Harlem tour with following gospel sermon in a church, and on Monday afternoon, we went to the airport and they flew back home to Germany. It was very exhausting, but I loved it. This was my beginning.

A very shocking experience I had on one tour. It was a Saturday when we flew into Buffalo to explore Niagara Falls. At La Guardia Airport, I gave all the people the boarding cards and told them to be at the gate forty-five minutes before departure. When we gathered at the gate, there was one person missing. I did not know who it was, because I did not know all the people yet. We boarded, and inside I counted again. That person still was missing. I told the flight attendant my misery. She let me get off the plane. They gave me a microphone at the gate, and I was able to announce in German that I was looking for…a missing person. Nothing happened. The pilot got involved, and he delayed the departure for ten minutes so that they could search the airport. I did not find that person. I realized again how helpful Americans are. This would never have happened in Germany. Everything was done by the rules. The pilot and the flight attendant would have done their job, but never would have gone out of their way like these two. The whole day, I was a nervous wreck. Late at night, when we came back to the hotel, there was an older woman sitting in the lobby. She came to me and excused herself. This was the missing person. I was surprised that she excused herself; I felt so guilty for not taking her along. But she felt guilty too. She did not speak English and was wandering around the airport to look at everything. She got lost and panicked; therefore, she did not hear my announcement over the loudspeaker. A young man who saw her anxiety and spoke German got her a cab and sent her back to the hotel. She was not upset with me, but this was a horror story for me.

Being with German visitors, I became very German again. I always shuffled myself ahead of everybody when we had to stay in line. I wanted to be the first. If something went wrong, I got angry with the person I had to deal with. I demanded to be served right away. I was not friendly at all and forgot what I had learned in America. My German people liked it and thought I was tough and I did a great job. I pushed and shuffled till one day it hit me. I was doing the opposite of what I had experienced in this country and what I admired the Americans for. From that point on, I changed. I actually told my people too to stay in line, be polite, never demand something, and be courteous to one another, as the Americans are. This was a change. My German friends learned another way of living. They liked it very much, and often they asked me why we couldn't be as friendly to each other in Germany. I achieved more this way too. American people went out of their way to help me, when before they ignored me.

Yes, they went out of their way. On planes, the flight attendants gave me the microphone to announce the menu in German. Or before we departed, I got the microphone to ask my people in German to board the plane. I often got asked, "Are you someone important? They treat you so special." Again, this was German thinking. "No, people help people in this country when you are polite" was my answer.

One day, I had a really great experience. We were flying American Airlines from La Guardia into Buffalo. Before arriving Buffalo, the voice of the pilot came on. He announced, "I just got an okay from the tower to fly over the falls for our German visitors. Would the tour guide please come into the cockpit to explain the falls? We've got ten minutes to do so." I was in that cockpit so fast, and here I was, between the pilot and the copilot with a microphone in my hands, explaining what the pilot was telling me about the beautiful Niagara Falls. We were right over them, and the view was overwhelming. The pilot made even a U-turn so the people on the other side of the plane could see it too. Ten minutes later, we arrived into Buffalo. There were businesspeople on the plane, but nobody complained. They actually cheered for the Germans, and yes, what the pilot did for the German group was overwhelming. My Germans did not believe that this was possible on a commercial airline. I was so thankful to the pilot. He was an ambassador for America. I hope he realized what he did. I learned again that if I am friendly and open-minded, I can turn the world around. This was so helpful in my job. I got more self-confidence from day to day.

Later on, when our children were older, I took jobs for two or three weeks, sometimes six weeks, taking German people all over the United States of America, where I had to give city tours, explain the parks, or explain the way of life. Germans wanted to know everything, even though they had prepared themselves by reading all kind of tour books before they came over. Besides those tours through the States and Canada, I did opera and art tours. I loved to fly and to stay in hotels. Through the years, I was able to pick those tours which I liked most and, sure, I choose the nicest and most expensive ones because hotels, airfares, and all activities were nicer.

Once I had another great experience. I had taken an opera tour. We were staying for three weeks in San Francisco to see the whole *Ring* cycle by Richard Wagner, which meant four operas per week three times over. I loved it very much. I had agreed to do it even though my Ingo would graduate from high school on the last day of these three weeks. No problem. My agent gave me a plane ticket back to New York one day earlier. This way, I was able to be with Ingo on the day of his graduation. The three weeks went by very fast, and a couple of days before my departure back home, I called the airline to reconfirm my flight. It was cancelled. I panicked. What shall I do? I called my agent in New York, and he got me another ticket from San Francisco via Houston into New York, arriving late at night, around eleven p.m. I was happy. When I boarded this flight in San Francisco, we had a one-hour delay. I only had forty-five minutes in Houston to catch the other flight. I got more and more nervous and, sure enough, when I arrived in Houston, my plane into New York was just pulling out. I could still see it. I went to the agent at the gate and begged him to bring the plane back. I told him about the graduation of my Ingo. I was a nervous wreck. I begged and begged. At first he said no, but then he felt sympathy for me, and he called the plane back to the gate. I jumped on, and I was thrilled. What a great agent this man was. I never, ever would have expected something like this. Again, I have to say people in this country are people with a heart.

When I checked in my people at the airport, the agents of all airlines always gave me a seat in the first-class section of the plane. I took it and liked it for a while, but then I stopped accepting it because my people thought either I was taking something away from them with their money or I was someone special. I didn't like either thing, and anyhow, I always was on a diet. I was not able to enjoy the good food and drinks in first class. On one flight from New York into Washington, I met the same flight attendant over and over again. A couple of times, she gave me potato chips and a bottle of wine at the end of the flight to relax in my hotel room after I got rid of all the people. Well, I gave it away to one of my people or a young couple, but what a nice way to treat me.

Having been away from Germany for years, now I realized that all my German tourists always were dressed alike. They always were wearing the latest fashion, so they all looked the same. Often I thought, "Wow, Mr. So-and-so is back" or "Mrs. So-and-so is still here," but it was someone else dressed like he or she was. I recall that I did the same when I lived in Germany. I bought the latest fashions to show the world I had the money and I was somebody. I felt terrible now and sad for my fellow Germans. Why weren't we Germans able to be ourselves and dress in our own style? For myself, I can say I was not myself, therefore I dressed after the latest fashion and thought this way I would get more recognition and people would like me more.

In America, I was able to wear everything I liked and not what was fashionable. I even got a compliment. I had tried this at the beginning of our stay. All my clothes I had collected over the years were still around. I was a packrat. Getting so many compliments on my wardrobe, I put on older and older clothes. The compliments did not stop. All of a sudden, I had so many clothes to wear because I was a packrat and had not thrown away my old clothes. I realized too that only the designer gets rich. It does not make me look better. I had to find my own style, and in this country, I was able to do so. My German visitors, being dressed up-to-date, were even taken by my wardrobe. If they had known how old everything was, they would have been in shock.

Another difference between German and American couples I noticed: a German couple sleeps in a king-size bed. The woman and man each have their own featherbed and pillow. My agency always ordered rooms with two beds. Sometimes there were one or two rooms with a king-size or queen-size bed because that was all the hotel had left. Every time this happened, the couple came down and complained. "How can we sleep with only one blanket and so close together?" Often I was able to change it, but sometimes not. Then I had to order another blanket for them. One girl at the registration of the Hyatt in Los Angeles once asked me, "Why do they not want to sleep close together? I always spoon with my husband." I realized there are two different worlds. I told my German visitors about these different customs at the beginning of our tour, and I did not get so many complaints anymore.

Checking into a hotel was usually very interesting. When I started to do these tours, people always surrounded me at the registration counter when I checked them in and went for the keys. There was a big flock around me. Not only was I embarrassed, but so was everybody else. I learned to tell them after a couple of tours to relax and just let me talk to the person at the registration. They obeyed like little children. This was good, because one time when we checked into the Park Hyatt Hotel in Santa Monica, California, no keys were ready for us. The hotel had forgotten to do this because they expected us the next day. We were lucky: they had enough rooms for us and, they worked urgently fast to fix this and get our keys ready. I acted like nothing had happened and told my people that it would take a little bit longer than usual because there was a convention going on. They relaxed and did not realize how fast people at the registration arranged to give us keys for nineteen rooms in a very short time. If my people had found out, I would have been in trouble. Thanks to American flexibility and friendliness, we got our keys. Even more, I realized how good and helpful it is without bureaucracy, which we Germans are used to.

Through all the years, I was hesitant to spend money. I felt guilty because I felt it was Heinz's money. Having been taught that it was important to have a good education so that I could earn my own money in case my husband died or I got divorced, I had a problem spending Heinz's salary after I stopped working in the beginning of our marriage and through all the years we were married. Heinz always told me it was *our* money and to feel free to spend it. He even gave me pocket money. It did not work. I felt guilty. Now, having a job, I earned money again. I was thrilled. For the first time, I felt that money gives you power. I had no problem spending the money I had made. Heinz was great. He told me to open my own account and put my money into it. This way, I was free to spend it wherever I wanted to. It really gave me a lot more freedom. Through the years, I bought three apartments and supervised these. It was fun. I was able to surprise the children and Heinz by buying big gifts. Before, when I was a housewife without a job, I never felt good when I bought a gift for Heinz with his own money. One thing I learned: money made me free, empowered me—not Heinz' money, but my own. I even was able to talk about it. It was a big step forward in my life. Looking around at some of my German friends, they still felt the burden of being not allowed to work—or, better said, their husbands told them, "You do not need to work!" Watching them, I could see that they were not happy because they were boxed in and not able to live up to their God-given gifts. One girlfriend especially: she had so many gifts as an interior decorator or gardener, but she "did not need to work." She spent her husband's money like crazy. It must have been a counter-attack.

Looking around at my German friends, I found out one thing. Most marriages were still husband-oriented. It was a power struggle. Husbands were workaholics, and the women were sick. Yes, husbands gave them whatever they wanted—things, but not the inner peace to become themselves. That must have been too scary. How did Don Miguel Ruiz describe it? "This is a war of control to see who will manipulate whom. Who will be the provider, and who will have the addiction? The respect is gone. You can see the resentment, the emotional poison, how they hurt each other, little by little, and it grows and grows, until they don't know when the love stops. They stay together because they are afraid to be alone, afraid of the opinions and judgments of others, and also afraid of their own judgments and opinions. But where is love? The one with the strongest will and less need won the war, but where is that flame they call love? They treat each other like possessions." He was right. Some pretended in front of everyone to be in love by kissing and putting on a show. They pretended to be in love because there was nothing behind it. It was a frame. American women are freer. In Germany, I recall how people were prejudiced, talking about American women who were the powerful ones in a family. The husbands were not chauvinistic enough. I learned that American women are a lot freer than German ones. Women's liberation started here, and it is great. I had a female psychologist once on a trip, and she agreed that America is ahead. I profited from this, and I was thankful. It is really the greatest country in the world, which offers freedom for everyone.

My father was a male chauvinist. He had all the say in the family. When I grew up, all the men in Germany were like that. If a man showed his feelings, he was stamped down as a sissy. My mother catered to my father. We had already been living in America for four years when he visited us for the first time. He overcame his fear of flying to see us. He was seventy-three years old, and it was his first time on a plane. He liked it very much and visited us again the next year. One day, I came home from shopping, and I heard someone playing our piano. I did not believe it. I silently sat down and listened. He did not realize I was around. After a while, he saw me and stopped promptly. Disturbed, he looked at me. I was not supposed to hear this. I was overwhelmed. I did not know that my father knew how to play the piano. He was very upset. I took him into my arms and let him know how surprised I was. "Why did you not let us know that you had this gift?" I asked him. For the first time in my life, I saw him crying. He said: "It is too late now." Three weeks later, back in Germany, he died. This was so sad. His whole life he was not able to be himself.

Another experience I had when I was working. One man in my opera group was a retired district attorney and judge. He spent his years listening to operas all over the world. Thirteen times he came over to the US. He was very much a male chauvinist. His wife had nothing to say; his children lived far away from him. When there were women doctors and women lawyers in the group, he always attacked them. He felt superior. In the beginning, I was afraid of him. He had written a book, and I got a copy. Yes, he showed himself in it as the greatest chauvinist there is. After years I got to his inner core and learned how soft he was.

One day, I had a Harlem tour in Manhattan, and we went to the Metropolitan Baptist Church in Harlem for a sermon. He was so touched by the people's belief in God. He took my hand, squeezed it, and said, "Why didn't you bring me over here sooner?" For the first time, I was able to look under his hard shell. Then, years later, I got a letter from him. He had not come for a couple of years to opera tours. He wrote me that he wanted to come again but was ashamed, because he was divorced and in love with a very nice lady. By then he was in his seventies. He came to New York. At the airport, he hugged me, and had he changed! He always was dressed very conservatively, in suits and ties. Now he was wearing jeans and a leather jacket. I did not believe this. In the back, there was a pretty woman. This was his new love. He had changed through her. He was no chauvinist anymore. They were in love and catered to each other. I was happy for both of them.

Heinz and I were struggling for real respect and love. We too had our problems. If I said something he did not like, he did not talk to me for hours or sometimes days. I did not like this, but I always had an excuse for him. His mother was a control freak and he was afraid to speak up. He went through a tough childhood because he was separated from his parents during the war and so on. I had all kinds of excuses till one day I watched the Oprah Show and learned that men who do this want to control their wives. After all these years, I had had it. I did not want to take it anymore. I went to counseling. This was a big step to make me free. In Germany, everybody thought all Americans "are lying on the coach," and everybody looked down on people who went for help. Here in America, it was okay. Actually, I learned from famous people who had gone for counseling how their lives had changed for the better. They were not afraid to admit this. You can improve your life by getting help. All sicknesses of the body start with a hurt soul. Those people who put counseling down are afraid to find out about themselves and rather depress their hurt feelings. Learning this, I loved to go for help. It was a big step forward. For the first time in my life, I got a good look inside myself and saw who I was. I had many issues. I was a perfectionist, an analyzer, and a pleaser. All my life, I was trying to please everyone but myself. Therefore, I had built up a lot of anger within me, which I did not show, but it came out sometimes when I was with people I trusted or when Heinz and I had a fight. Otherwise, I always had to be Mrs. Nice.

With all this anger in me, I was not a happy person. Another eye-opener was…I had problems with sex. Being raised very Catholic, sex for me was always a sin when I was growing up. When I was a little girl or teenager, we lived not far away from a restaurant where they had dancing on weekends. It was very romantic. The dance floor was on the bank of a river, and everything was lit by candles. On the street, there were couples standing on the corner kissing one day when my mother and I went home. "Look at those cheap girls, how they throw themselves away," I heard her saying. I was so uptight, and even when I was married, I still waited for Heinz to come and start loving me. I never, ever would have started anything, and I never would have said, "No, I am not in the mood." I did not know I was allowed to have fun too. As a wife, I had to be ready whenever the husband wanted it. Never do it for myself. Through counseling, I learned I have the right to do what I like to do and enjoy it. What a change.

Learning that I am an analyzer was surprising to me. I thought everybody always takes apart each situation or everybody always wants to learn about other people. This was not the case. Only some people are analyzers like me. Therefore, I was questioning everything and everyone when I came into this country. It was helpful.

I felt so good to learn about myself and started to change. One of the first books my counselor gave me to read was *The Dance of Anger* by Harriet Lerner. It fit. After a couple of months, Heinz joined me. At first, he did not like it, but when he saw how I changed to become more myself, we both went together. Like many partners, we both were pushed into certain roles within our marriage and now were allowed to explore ourselves. We learned a new way to communicate with each other. My anger went away. I learned self-respect. I started hard to work on my "pleaser." Even today, I have trouble overcoming it. Once, a girlfriend had her parents over, and I invited them. Her father was supposed to play cards with Heinz around one p.m. I had a dentist appointment and would not be back till three p.m. I asked my girlfriend to come with her mother at three p.m. She is a great soul, but sometimes very fresh, or even very German. She told me that they would be there at one p.m. Normally, I would not have said anything, but now, working on my pleaser, I told her "Please come at three p.m. when I am back from the dentist. I want to be there when I have friends over." This was so hard for me to do, but when I talked to my counselor, she told me it was okay always to do what I feel is right for me. More and more, I started to work on this. It felt good afterwards. People were not able anymore to take advantage of me. But another time, I chickened out. This girlfriend, who is very controlling, turned off the lights in my house. I always have the lights on. I hate darkness. I turned them on again, but behind my back, she turned them off. We had more friends around, and I did not say anything or do anything. But this did not feel good, because somebody took advantage of me. I am still learning.

In America, you give a compliment when you acknowledge something nice about a person. If you see something you do not like, you keep your mouth shut. Not so in Germany. It is called being honest. You tell your best friend even negative things.

Recently, I had bought myself a very nice pair of shoes. They were light blue and open in the back. It was January, but it was seventy-eight degrees Fahrenheit. I was wearing these shoes, and a German girlfriend who was over looked at me and said, "Oh my, what kind of shoes are you wearing? We don't have summer yet." I answered: "I always have summer." Again, no American friend would say something like that, but being German you always tell the truth, nothing but the truth. As a German, hearing some negative remarks like that, I always went into counter attack. With my American friends, getting compliments, I feel very good and my self-esteem grows.

Once, I had a luncheon with a German girlfriend and Americans. We talked about her mother-in-law who is twenty years older than I am. She told me, "My mother-in-law is not as wrinkled as you." My American friends were shocked. How could somebody say something like that? I used to be the same. We even say more negative things to people than positive ones. We think we are helping the other person to overcome her negative attitude. We do not see that we put down a person and make that person feel miserable. It was amazing how all of us Germans were raised the same. We never learned to say "Thank you" after we get a compliment. We are not used to it. I have a lot of German girlfriends who have lived in this country for years. If you give them a compliment, they turn it down. Recently, I told one girlfriend, "You are wearing a beautiful dress" The answer was, "Oh, no, it is two years old." After all those years, I too have to overcome this feeling to say those simple words, "Thank you." What did Billy Graham say? "Let's take the things that set us apart, that make us different, which cause us to disagree, and make them an occasion to compliment each other and be thankful for each other. Let us be big enough to be smaller than our neighbor, spouse, friends, and strangers. We would all live more comfortably with everybody around us if we would find the strength in being grateful and happily incompatible."

The "old Ulla" knew how other people had to behave, what they had to do. I had the answer for everything and everyone. It is easier to fix the faults of other people than those of myself, I realized. There's an old saying: "It's a lot easier to spot the flea on someone else's shoulder than to see the elephant on your own." Today, I realize I was a control freak. I wanted to have power over others because I had no power over myself. Today, I try to look into myself and tell myself what to do. I do not even take this behavior from other people anymore. One German girlfriend does the same things I did. Talking to her feels like looking into the mirror. She knows everything (she thinks) and told me constantly what to do. I only had to mention something; she had the answer. At one point, I told her I did not want her judgment, but that of a professional. She got the message, and today we have a great relationship.

I still recall one incident when I started to work: one man told me, "Mrs. Reichhardt, you know everything. Whenever you get asked something, you have an answer." I was so proud of myself. Through the years, then, I learned I was not humble enough. I was afraid to say, "I do not know, but I will look it up." In Germany, you have to know everything. I was afraid to get judged by people and to be looked down on as being dumb. The intellect counts more than the emotion of a person. In America, it is more important to be yourself. You are allowed to be what you are, even to make mistakes.

In America, we also learned that you have to start planning early for your retirement. Heinz did this. He went into the stock market so we would have a good life when we were retired. After having a job—I mentioned it before—I bought three apartments and went into the stock market. In Germany, you were insured by the government. You got a pension after you retired, which was high enough to live on and always had health-insurance. You did not have to worry. We learned to take care of ourselves in our new chosen country, even though it took us some years.

More and more, I became Americanized. Once, being back in Germany, I realized that I saw differences which I had never seen before. People were not as free in their own way of thinking as in the US. Everybody tried to do what was in or expected from them to do. One time, corn was introduced as a vegetable. I got served corn wherever I went. Another time, in the seventies, they started to grill, as we had learned in America. Everybody was grilling now. Everybody wanted to impress other people.

Visiting my sister and brother-in-law, I became German again. During one stay, Kirsten asked for ketchup. I yelled at her to stop this, because I knew that Germans think Americans eat a lot of ketchup, which is so unhealthy, and they look down on this. Deep down, I did not want them to think that way. Kirsten, on the other hand, was shocked. She did not know why I acted like this. Today, I would not do this. I learned again that it takes a while to change. Then my brother-in-law talked about a colleague, another doctor.

He said, "By now, he should have his own house and not live in an apartment!" With my American attitude, I thought, "It is not his problem. If his friend is happy with his apartment, it is his friend's decision, not my brother-in-law's." I realized that all people still talked about other people. Exactly the way I was raised. I would have been the same years ago, thought like that and talked like that. Wow, did I change into an American.

I loved to gossip. I was raised that way. Gossiping made me feel superior to the other person. It felt good, and I always felt right about my own point of view. But this was only in the moment. In the long run, I felt more miserable about myself. I was learning that gossip reflects the insecurity of those who initiate it. When I make a negative statement about others behind their back, I do so because I want to feel powerful—and that's usually because I in some way I feel powerless, unworthy, not courageous enough to be forthright. Hurtful words also send the message, both to ourselves and to those with whom we share them, that we can't be trusted. I learned through the years and counseling, if someone is willing to tear down one "friend," why wouldn't she be willing to disparage another? Gossip means we haven't emboldened ourselves to talk directly to the people we take issue with, so we belittle them. In short, gossip is an assassination attempt by a coward like me. People have their own lives to worry about. I have to worry about myself. I was on my way to loving myself. This way, I had no need anymore to gossip about others.

Better than tearing down others through gossip is building our own dreams. This I heard once from Oprah. She was another woman in this country I admired from the moment I saw her, and still admire. She too taught me a lot. It was the beginning of 1980s in Chicago. I had an opera group coming over from Germany.

While I was waiting for them, I turned on the television, and here was this black woman by the name of Oprah. She had a talk show and was interviewing Elisabeth Kuebler-Ross. I had read her book, *On Death and Dying,* and was glued to the television. In the beginning, Elisabeth Kuebler-Ross was an atheist but became a believer by watching the dying over years. She had taught us to talk about death when one of our loved ones is dying. She also had taught us that we go through five stages of grief: denial, anger, bargaining, depression, and acceptance. She was a pioneer. This was my start with Oprah. Later, when she became national, I tried always to watch her when I had time and she had a good topic. I learned so much through her. Judgmental as I used to be, I became aware how terrible this is. Oprah introduced me to all the subjects I never had heard about, like battered women, homosexual people, the homeless. I became more understanding to all these people. I felt compassion. In Germany, I was raised with the idea that "You have character," what meant you never change. Here, I learned to change and to accept everyone. Changing was a process of growing. If I have never walked in the shoes of others, who am I to judge?

I will never forget when Oprah once told us the first time she saw Sidney Poitier, she made up her mind: "I want to be like him." She was nine years old, and she followed her dream. Often, I asked myself what would have happened if I had been raised in America and had been able to live out my inner gifts. Well, I was able to change now; there was still time to do so.

Through all of these thoughts, for the first time, I understood what "the American dream" meant. In school, I had learned that in America, there were busboys who made it to become millionaires. But I thought this was years ago. Living in this country, I realized it still was happening every day. Whatever you are, whatever you feel, can become reality, because you are not stuck in a certain kind of thinking. You do not get judged. Society makes you free to fulfill your potential. This was overwhelming for me. There were Siegfried and Roy in Las Vegas, Wolfgang Puck and Arnold Schwarzenegger in Los Angeles, and a lot more. They all had come over to America at the same time we had, and look what had happened to them. They used the gifts God had given to them. They allowed themselves to be themselves. I realized there were so many more entrepreneurs around. They used their God-given gifts. I recall once I was in Austria, visiting a girlfriend, asking her about Arnold Schwarzenegger. She told me that people still looked down on him because he came from nothing. By then, he was a movie star and no governor. Even when Ronald Reagan became president, my German people talked about that "cowboy." Here in America, nobody is ashamed when he comes from a poor background—the opposite: everybody is proud to have made it. This is the only country in the world where things like this happen.

Growing into the American way of thinking, I changed a lot. I was raised never, ever to do a low-paying job, and when I was going to school, I never was allowed to work. Heinz was different— again, more American. He encouraged our children to work when they were in school. They started delivering newspapers, cleaning pots and pans at an Italian diner, selling food and clothes in an apartment store. At first, it was hard for me to give in to this, but over the years I was thankful to Heinz and America. During the time when our children had these low-paying jobs, I went to Germany to visit my beloved aunt in Bonn. When she learned that our children were working in these jobs, she was upset and asked me: "Are you financially in trouble? Don't you want to come back to Germany?" She certainly did not understand. Children learn from the beginning what it means to work in all kinds of jobs and become open-minded later on to low-paying jobs and feel sympathy for people of all levels. People are not conceited and do not look down to other people. The only thing that counts is that you have to perform.

Yes, I too changed drastically. When I started to work as a tour guide, it was unthinkable for me to get a tip. I was ashamed. I will never forget the first time it happened. My colleague Glen and I had worked for four days together with a large group of people. For both of us, it was our first job. It was 1978. Glen was a nice African American guy from Brooklyn who had studied in Munich and had learned the German language while in the army. We brought our people to Kennedy Airport, checked them in, and said "Goodbye." Everyone came over and gave us a tip. Glen was happy and thanked them. I was ashamed and said, "Please, no." I was wearing a pantsuit with pockets all over. When I did not want to take the money, our guests put it into my pockets. I said *"No"* when they gave me the money, but it felt good when I had it. What a different feeling. Glen and I went into the next bar to share the tips. Here I took the money out of all my pockets: the left side of my jacket, then the right side, and then of the left pocket of my pants, and then the right pocket of my pants. I put it all in front of us. Glen got all his money out. We counted it together and then wanted to share it. All of a sudden, I realized that the barkeeper was watching us. He had a funny face. Today, I think I know what he thought. This was my first chance to appreciate tips. When I came home, the whole family had fun with it. Kirsten and Ingo helped me to count all the dollars, and I felt so good sharing some with them. I started to like money.

I think I started to build my own dream. I loved my job very much. I became more aware of myself and did what I loved to do. I loved people. I was outgoing noisy in order to learn about people. I loved staying in nice hotels, flying, and arranging things. When I sat on an airplane taking off, I was thrilled and got a feeling like all bad stuff stayed behind me on earth. Here I am free like a bird. I felt wanted.

The beginning of these long tours through the USA and Canada were very hard. I had to go to a lot of seminars again. I always was scared to death when I brought people to places I had never been to. I studied through the night till three or four in the morning.

Through all the years I was working—nineteen all together—I only had two women who were nasty. This was when I first started to work. I still recall the first time a woman was nasty to me. I had never been in Ottawa and had to give a city tour. I studied and studied. Going towards the Parliament building, we went by the Rideau River and the Rideau Canal. I explained everything about these rivers, but then there was a third one. I did not read up about a third one. I was in shock when this woman asked me, "Mrs. Reichhardt, what is this river?" I did not know. After we had checked into the hotel, she knocked at my door and told me, "I sent my husband to find out what the third river was. It was the Rideau Canal. You gave us wrong information." I was ashamed. What did I do? Well, the Rideau River had two arms, which I had overlooked. I learned my lesson.

The second woman was very nasty to me. On one trip, I changed the route going through Virginia to Florida because we had a blizzard. I took Highway 95, which was safer. I did this after I had asked all the people on the bus. This woman now went to everyone afterwards and told them that we had missed out on the most interesting places. She tried to get the other people on her side. So I concentrated on her and tried to be very nice to her, told her that we did not miss a lot, etc., but she kept up her nasty work. After a while, I realized people were not listening to her anymore, and I gained their confidence back. She was alone with her turmoil. She did not like herself and was a troublemaker. Otherwise, during all the nineteen years, all the people were nice. We always felt like a family after a while.

On the first tours I ever did, I was so shy I could not face the people when I was talking on the microphone. I was hiding myself on the bus when I picked them up from the airport and gave them a big welcome explaining everything. Through the years, I became less self-conscious, but still the beginning of each tour was terrible, through all the years I was working. I was a nervous wreck. I had nightmares. Heinz was so sweet. He called this "stage fright." The first day, when I faced the people, I looked into those faces which were friendly. I tried very hard to get through to the people. Some looked at me as if to say, "What does she have to offer?" They had paid a lot of money and wanted the best of the best. Everyone had prepared themselves, and there were people from all backgrounds. The more expensive the tour was, the more educated they were. How could I tell them something? But after two or three days, when I called home, Heinz told me, "Now you have established good communication and relationships with all of them!" Yes, he was right. He was able to learn this by the way I was talking. I sounded relaxed. I had overcome my own fear and felt wanted.

Opera tours I liked very much. When I grew up in Germany, I never was allowed to go to the movies: "only uneducated people went there." My mother took me to the opera and plays of Schiller or Shakespeare, etc., where educated people went. How prejudiced to write this down now, with my American thinking. In Texas, a girlfriend once told me, "Old people like operas; we like rock and roll." In my early years, I was not interested in opera at all, but I had to go with my mother. I was always waiting for the intermission to meet friends and was happy when it was over. I saw or heard quite a lot of operas and started to like them.

Having this job as a tour guide, I got tours from the only opera agency in New York. German-speaking people came over to the USA for one or two weeks to go to the opera. When they came for only one week, our group went to the Met every night. I had to bring them there and stay with them. I loved this. I stayed with them in a hotel in Manhattan. I had to do everything: give them a reception after arriving, a city tour, a trip to a musical on Broadway, concerts at Carnegie Hall or Avery Fisher Hall. I had to bring them through the museums, mostly the Metropolitan Museum of Art or the Museum of Modern Art, and sometimes the Guggenheim or the Frick. We went to the best restaurants. I was glad that I had heard so many operas in Germany growing up. Sometimes, I had to give them an introduction, even though they knew more than I did. After the city tour, we often had lunch at the "Windows of the World" at the World Trade Center.

Once, I had a gentleman from Switzerland. He told me he was not able to come along for the city tour, but he would meet us at the restaurant because at home he had a butler and now he has to dress himself, which will take a long time. When I met him after the city tour, I was in shock. He was dressed in jeans, with a sweatshirt and a trench coat. The "Windows of the World" had a dress code. I told the manager my problem, and he let him in, but he was not allowed to go up to the buffet, and he was given a jacket which he had to wear. My friend was upset. I told him, "Look at home you have a butler; here, I am your butler and I will get for you everything you like from the buffet." He agreed.

When opera groups came over for more than one week, we stayed four days in Manhattan, then flew to Chicago to experience the Lyric Opera and then to San Francisco to the War Memorial Opera. I liked these tours so much because we did everything which used to be hobbies of mine. I loved museums, theater, books, operas, restaurants, hotels, airplanes and people. On top of it, I had to manage everything. This was a lot easier in this country than it would have been in Germany. Everybody again was friendly and helpful. I started to feel important. My self-esteem grew. I became a happier person.

Once, I had a group with an escort. He was very important to us, because he brought a lot of people over. He was president at the travel department of the ADAC, which is an equivalent to AAA. Flying American Airlines, I asked politely if they can seat him in first class. No problem. They did on all flights. He was thrilled. Then at Lufthansa, the German airline, I did the same and was told, "No, sorry. You have to apply for this four weeks ahead at the headquarters in Germany in writing." What a difference!

Another time, we were in Los Angeles when a woman came upset to my room. Someone had stolen her purse. I went with her to the police station to report this. She wanted something in writing for her insurance. The police gave it to her, but she insisted on having this paper stamped. The policeman smiled and asked, "Why?" Well, in Germany it would not have been accepted without a stamp. Bureaucracy is still around in the old country. Everything has to be 100%.

In the meantime, I had learned that I could get around just by being friendly and not so demanding. That was so helpful. I was able to turn the world around. When we boarded an airplane, the flight attendant gave me the microphone to announce the meals in German, or I was able to call them for boarding at the gate in German, and we were allowed to board ahead of everybody else, which was very helpful for me, because I found out right away when a person was missing. My German people, who were used to all the bureaucracy, thought that I was somewhat important, but I told them with friendliness you can turn the world around over here. They were very impressed.

We often stayed in the St. Moritz Hotel at Central Park in New York. Before we checked in, I got asked if they should hang out the German flag for the group. I accepted this gratefully. When my German guests arrived, they asked me, "What important person is here from Germany?" When I told them that it was for them, they were surprised that people of a hotel were doing this.

When I came to this country, I was afraid that I never would be able to survive if something happened to Heinz. I was educated in Germany and had worked in Germany. How would I be able to work here or support the children? One time, Heinz and I saw an opera at the Met, and I thought, "Maybe I can become a toilet-woman if something like that should happen. I love operas, and I could hear them for free." Yes, I heard them for free, but with a job I really loved. Over and over, I learned this country is open to everyone. Everybody has a chance—even I do. Through my job, I met so many people of all backgrounds, in all situations, and I was able to assess the difference between the German and American people.

Recently, my sister spent a week with us in Florida. I realized she still was the way we were raised. She was afraid to show her emotions. When I gave her a compliment, she turned it down by saying, "It is nothing…it is old…etc." I told her I had learned here in America to say "thank you." She is very sweet, and I love her, but I did not tell her this because I would have upset her. When we parted at the airport, we both cried, and she said, "How stupid that I am crying!"

I told her *"No,* it is great that you show how sad you are." She was ashamed to show her feelings.

After she had been back in Germany for a couple of weeks, we were talking on the phone when she told me, "Americans are superficial. They never criticize anything. For them, everything is beautiful." She had watched us when the children and I said, "I love you," gave each other compliments, etc. I told her how this country has changed me and how much easier it is to take a positive step in life. I told her that I have learned in the USA that our EQ is as important—maybe even more—than our IQ, and that I learned to show my emotion. Was I blessed to be here!

My relationship with my children was so different too. For years, I'd almost driven myself crazy trying to change Kirsten and Ingo into the people I felt they could be, or better said, into my beliefs. My excuse was that I loved them so much. I just wanted them to become what I thought was good for them. Finally, I faced up to the deeper truth: there is only one person I'll ever be able to change—myself! Interestingly enough, though, the positive changes I have the courage to make in myself will affect those around me. Today, we love each other and show it. I never end a phone call without saying, "I love you." I am not that nerve-racking mother who tells them what to do anymore. Sure, they are adults, but I had learned to love them for what they are and not what I wanted them to be. This is so great. We share our feelings—what a difference from my sister—and became closer and closer, even though they went their own ways in life. I adore them. It was a long way to learn this, but it is never too late, I realized. What did Mahatma Gandhi say? *"You must be the change you want to see in the world."*

I wrote about all the good things happening to me in this country. Being a full fledged American now I got very much hurt, when the USA had his darkest day and I was parat of it. Kirsten worked for SunMicrosystem. Her office was in the World Trade Center on the 26. floor in Tower 2. In June of 2001 Heinz and I visited her. She wanted to show us her office. We had to go through so much security. They took a photo of us, gave each of us a badge, then we got screened, not once but 2 or 3 times. When last not least we were able to take the elevator upstairs we only were allowed up to the 25th floor. A receptionist called Kirsten down and then she had to bring us upstairs to her office. After all of this I never will forget the sentence I told her "You are in the safest place on earth",. How wrong was I!

On September 11, 2001 here in Houston I had my TV on watching the "Today Show" while straitening out our bedroom. All of a sudden I heard Katie Couric announcing, that a plane just hit the World Trade Center Tower 1. It was 8.45 a.m. I calmed myself down by telling me, that it must have been a commercial plane, which hit the tower by accident. This happened July 1945 to the Empire State Building, when a bomber crashed into the building at the 78th and 79th floor. Building the WTC they took this under consideration. I started to worry about Kirsten. She usually is always late in the morning, so I called her at home. No answer! Was she already at work? I called her there…no answer, then I called her cell. phone…..no answer. I panicked! One minute I told myself she is in Tower 2 not Tower 1, the next minute I saw her killed. Then I watched when the 2nd plane hit Tower 2. I started to count the floors. Now I knew something terrible had happened, en on TV they talked about terrorists. After 3 minutes, when the 2nd plane hit, my phone was ringing. It was Kirsten "Mom, do you know what's going on?"

she screamed. "Yes, where are you" was my answer. "I am out" then we got disconnected. I tried and tried again to reach her, but there was no phone service anymore. These were the darkest minutes of my life. One minute I thought she made it out and then I got scared again that she did not really make it. Last not least around 11 o'clock that morning she called. She was safe already at the apartment of a girl friend on the Upper East Side.

Later I learned that she had been in the office early in the morning at 7 a.m., because she had to give a presentation. A colleague had seen, when Tower 1 got hit and came yelling through the office "Get out, there has been a explosion". It was 8.50 a.m. Kirsten looked out of her window and saw thousands of sheet papers falling from the sky. Some of them were on fire. She and a coworker started to run down the staircase, pushed themselves through security, who tried to prevent them from going outside, but they did it anyhow and ran down Liberty Street. When they hit Broadway the 2nd plane crashed into Tower 2. They ran and ran and then called home. That was, when I got her first phone call. She really was out and safe.

But the days after were very shocking. We were constantly on the phone. She was in shock and did not want to leave her colleagues, who all made it out safe. I wanted her to come home to Houston, but not plane, train or bus was leaving Manhattan. After a couple of days she was able to take a Greyhound bus to Houston and even found out after hours on the bus, that planes out of North Carolina were leaving again. She switched from bus to plane and got to Houston. Again she did not find peace. She wanted to go back to Manhattan after a week and go back to work. I flew with her to keep her company.

The next day we walked downtown to Ground Zero. Coming to Canal Street everything was closed off. We went over to Broadway and marched south. It became eerie and smoky. We didn't talk, but marched. A lot of people were doing the same Nobody talked, some cried, most had very stony faces. Everybody was eager to see reality. Then we came to St. Paul's Chapel and were able to look down the street. We used to see the World Trade Center there, but there was nothing. Sadness filled our hearts. On the next block we saw debris and a wall standing from what used to be the WTC. We hugged each other and cried. A policeman came towards us and said "Ladies, you are not allowed to be here, but take your time". We went to Liberty Street and up the steps of Chase Manhattan Bank. Here we were able to look down and saw even more of that terrible mess. We were used to see this beautiful building right over there and now it was ashes, debris and still smoke coming out. All of a sudden Kirsten became stiff. It was too much for her. She sat down, got her cell. phone out and arranged a meeting in N.J. with a customer. It took a while. I did not know how to help or comfort her. When we left, we went down Liberty Street towards the East River. This was where Kirsten ran on Sept. 11. She started talking again, explaining how they ran and what they were thinking. They were afraid the Towers would fall down on them and therefore they ran and wanted to jump into the East River. She talked and talked. After a while I reminded her, that we were going into the wrong direction. We turned around and went north. At City Hall Kirsten sat down at the fence, got her cell. phone out and talked business again. There was a policeman in front of City Hall. I asked him, if he wants to hear a story. "I heard so many stories these days, what is it?" "Have a look" I told him "my daughter had her office in the WTC on the 26th floor. Now she is doing business here at the fence of the Mayors office". "Well I thought, I had heard it all, but this is different and new" was his answer.

Then we went by a fire station, there were photos all over of all the firemen, who died while doing their job. Flowers, teddy bears, bows and flags were all over. 2 firemen were standing outside with faces totally numb. We talked to them and hugged them. All of a sudden it seemed like we all were a big family. We all were hurt so much and felt the same. But my Kirsten was alive and given to me the second time.

It was and still is such an American tragedy. They wanted to harm America, the American people and I was one of them, who really too got hit hard. Being back in Houston I made a poem for Kirsten, to let all the hurt out. Here it is:

OUR WORLD TRADE CENTER

Our hearts are broken with all the pain
I really think I am becoming insane.

When I took the test to become a tour guide
I had to learn about New York City with all his pride
I loved that city with all my heart
To learn about the World Trade Center was the greatest part
Minoru Yamasaki had that great idea
To built something worth for this world right here
It showed us everything America believed in
Prosperity, greatness and God from within!

It stood right there on the Hudson River
From its top you experienced the world with its glimmer
I brought all the Germans up and spread my love
For that New York City right from above!

The observation deck opened really your mind
Nowhere else were you able to see this kind
You see the ocean, the mountains and right into the heart
Of New York City's greatest part.

Central Park - 5th Avenue - the Empire State Building were there
I felt like you could touch it all from where we were
And the Statue of Liberty, the greatest Lady of all
Stood beneath there - guiding the bay - stood firm and tall
Greeting all ships, which came in from far away
Letting people know "You are welcomed here our
   American way".

Then there was this glamorous restaurant on top of Tower 1
Called "Windows of the World" on the 107th floor it was done.
From here you experienced the World as a haven
And nowhere else were you closer to heaven.
From here you had the greatest view
And the food they served was delectable too.

I loved this building the greatest on earth
Which was created to give us great worth.

My daughter - my Kirsten - got an office right there
On the 26th floor, how proud I was for her
She must be so blessed to work from this latter
Creating through her job everything even better.

But then all my pride went berserk one day
When September 11 those bustards had their SAY.
They crashed a plane first into Tower 1
And then another into Tower 2, where my Kirsten was one
Who was innocent only doing her job
And these killers tried to take her away and rob
Everything we were proud of - believed in and even our life
They took it all in a second - Thank God Kirsten survived.

She worked this day early on the 26th floor
Was in her office didn't open her door
Till a colleague came running yelling out loud
"Get out here. They will kill you without a doubt".

I saw on TV in Texas this mess
Prayed to God, asked him please do Kirsten bless.
Then another Plane crashed into Tower # 2
That's where my LOVE was and I died too
The seconds were long - the minutes were scary
But then Kirsten called "Mom, I am out of it - it's eerie".

Then the phones all went dead - The day was long
To God I prayed and my prayers were strong.
HE heard me and listened and made it worth
He gave my Kirsten the second birth
And now it was even more beautiful than the first one
Because I knew her and loved her for a very long run.

We found each other again in this world
And both learned a lot of what really is worth
I flew to N.Y. we both went down to "Ground Zero"
Saw the rest of our dream all destroyed by these weirdoes.

We hugged eachother together we cried
Even a policeman buried his dream and his pride
He hugged us and asked in a very soft voice
"Are you o.k. ladies? Take your time and rejoice"
He comforted us in all this mess
There still were people with a big heart in their chest.

Again and again we saw people who were hurt
In these couple of seconds their world was in a blurt.

Especially one fire station was decorated great
On top were 9 photos of the Best who had died
Underneath the photos were flowers, candles and flags
2 living guys stood outside their uniforms showed the tags
Their faces were dead without any sign
We hugged them - we cried - will this world ever be fine?

Ulla Reichhardt

I loved New York City and the WTC was my pride
But I almost lost Kirsten - my best one - my light.
Therefore my heart really cries out loud
DEAR GOD HELP US - WE NEED YOU MORE THAN
  EVER - ON THIS ROAD
LET US SEE YOU MORE DEEPLY - YOUR BEAUTY
  - YOUR LOVE
YOU ONLY GIVE LIGHT AND HARMONY FROM ABOVE
LET PEACE COME BACK INTO OUR HURTING HEARTS
AND NEVER EVER SET US APART
FROM YOU WITH ALL YOUR LOVE AND BEAUTY
ON THIS EARTH LET US LEARN OUR DUTY
LET US ALL AS A FAMILY AND A NATION COME BACK
TO YOU AND SEE YOUR GOOD WILL ON OUR TRACK
LET US HEAL OUR WOUNDS IN YOUR GREAT SPIRIT
AND FEEL THE GOOD IN THESE HURTING MINUTES
LET US REJOICE - GIVE MORE LOVE ON THIS EARTH
WHICH WILL BRING US TO YOU - WHERE WE WILL
  SEE OUR WORTH

My Relationship with God

Often I have mentioned that I was raised Catholic. My mother was Catholic, the oldest of eight children; my father, Lutheran. My grandparents on my mother's side were both very Catholic. When my parents were dating, I learned later on, they were not allowed to do so because my father was Lutheran. My grandfather even spat at him. But they did get married, and I never found out what it took for them to do so. Naturally, my sister and I became Catholic.

As a little child, I recall having to go to church every morning. It was a sin if I did not go. My mother made me go. I was so little that I hardly was able to look over the bench, and I asked God to let me grow faster. When I was around ten years old, I went to a children's mass every Sunday at nine o'clock. My mother had gone earlier, so as to be home to get me ready, and my father slept in. When he got up around ten or eleven o'clock, he was singing and a very happy person. I felt sorry for him. He sinned by not going to church, and I prayed for him. I confronted him once and begged him to come along to church, but his answer was, "I find God in his beautiful nature." Yes, he loved to hike, and almost every Sunday, the two of us walked for miles and ended up in a restaurant, where I got an apple cider and a sandwich and he had his beer and a sandwich. In those days, I liked the last part, being in a restaurant, more than the hike; but through it, I learned to love hiking more and more, and even today, I love it. Heinz and I did a lot of hiking when the children were young.

As a Catholic, I had to pray in the morning when I got up, at night before I went to sleep, and before every meal. It was a sin not to do so. So I prayed. I was afraid I would forget a prayer, and so as not to be punished by God, I overdid it. At night, I said thirteen prayers at one time, I remember. I wanted to be on the sure side, so as not to become a sinner. I read a lot of books, and I liked the ones about the martyrs, who became saints and went right to heaven. They were on the sure side when they died, while I was such a sinner, and who knows? I prayed to God to give me a terrible sickness before I died, like cancer or something else where I would really have to suffer. Then I would be sure of being saved and going to heaven and not to hell, where I did not want to end up.

When I was ten years old, I had my first communion. I went to confession before it; I had to. It was the first time I did not feel like a sinner anymore. It really made me feel good, and on my special day, I was so happy from within. I received God. He was with me. A photo was taken by the photographer to remember this great day. I was afraid to smile. Living in the Black Forest a couple of years ago, where people were very Catholic, I had learned it was a sin to smile in the communion photo. So I looked very serious for a ten-year-old child. We had a little party. Relatives came over, and I got gifts. I was wearing a big golden cross with a pearl. It was from my great-grandmother. From a neighbor, I got a bag of potatoes, and I was happy. Yes, it was 1947, and we did not have enough food. Germany was just recovering from the war. I recall that every morning, when we came home from church, we toasted a slice of bread on the stove and ate it without anything on it. For dinner, we had parsnips cooked in water without anything in it. To this day, I cannot eat parsnips anymore. I tried once to cook a meal with this vegetable, but it reminded me of those early days when we were so hungry.

I went to Catholic school till I was ten years old. Then I took the test to go to the "Gymnasium" (high school), where students from all denominations were together. Then we only had to go to church before school started twice per week. Once I sinned: I went with my Lutheran friend to her church. I wanted to see what it was like. I got punished for that when my mother found out. She had promised when she got married to raise her children Catholic; otherwise she would not have been able to get married in the Catholic church..

When I was in church, I prayed and prayed as I had learned, but I did not get too much out of it. The mass was in Latin, and I did not understand a word. In my prayer book, it was translated, but it was hard work. Yet, through the years, I memorized all the prayers. High mass was long. It took more than an hour. I was glad when it was over, but in those days, I never would have admitted this, because it would have been a sin again. The priest from his pulpit always reminded us what sinners we were and how we could become better. I did not want to be that sinner and went to confession every week. After that, I felt good again.

In this way, I grew up. On Sundays, I went to church all my life. During the time I was growing up in Germany, less and less people went to church. Actually, at one point, people looked down on those who still were committed. Especially, intelligent people looked down on churchgoers. "Only the old and dumb people were going to church" was the opinion of the masses. But I was afraid not to go. I did not want to burn in purgatory or hell.

We learned, and even prayed in the "Credo" during mass, that the Catholic Church was the only one to help you to go to heaven. Was I lucky to be born into this church and not into another one! I felt sorry for all the people of different faiths—not only other Christians, but what about the Buddhists, Muslims, Hindus, Jews and so on? I was anxious to find out what happened to them. When I was in my teens, I read books about other religions. They believed very strongly too. I prayed to God to send the Holy Spirit to teach me and open my mind. I came up with the idea that God revealed himself to us humans in that faith we understand the most, surrounded by different customs and attitudes. There is only one God. But I still wanted to be on the safe side, and I practiced my Catholic religion.

When I fell in love with Heinz, I had to go through a big test. He was Lutheran; well, my father was too, so my parents were okay with this. After we had dated for some time, we talked marriage. One day Heinz told me that, in order to get married to him, I had to convert to the Lutheran faith. That was a shock for me. It was not only a shock—it was a sin in my belief system. He gave me three days to think it over. I never will forget those three days. It was torture. I loved him very much. He was the right guy for me, whom I would love enough to be married to, but giving up my Catholic religion? How was I able to survive? I would live in sin. He always was very tolerant, but now… I did not sleep for three nights. After this time, I had the solution. No, as much as I loved him, my afterlife was more important. I wanted to go to heaven when I died. We met. I told him, crying, that I was not able to marry him, even though I loved him very much. He looked at me and said: "If it is so important to you, let's get married anyhow!" Did I hear right? Was that his answer? I didn't believe it. Here I was, struggling for days with a question of life and death, and then very easily, without thinking, he answered me like that. I was confused. How could he do this to me? He was never even raised in any confession, only baptized Lutheran. He always was looking for a religion and was taken by his best friend, whose father was a preacher. He belonged to the reformed Lutheran church in that village where Heinz grew up. He was Heinz' idol, and therefore Heinz wanted to be like him. We talked and talked for hours. I overcame my shock, and then we decided to get married. Heinz only made one statement and told me, "Never ever bring me a black guy home." This was the name Catholic priests were called in Germany. I promised it, and we both wanted to stick to our faiths.

Well, then we had to go through another step. In order for me to stay Catholic, I had to get married in the Catholic Church. After having a hard time talking it over, we went to the Catholic pastor of my home church, where I was baptized and still belonged to, when I visited my parents. As everyone might think, Heinz did not like this, but he did it for me. He learned that *he* had to raise the children we would have in the Catholic faith. Again, he had to overcome a burden, but it looked as if he got used to it. He promised to do so.

We got married. Usually when getting married in the Catholic Church, you have a mass, which includes the wedding ceremony. Not so with us. Because Heinz was Lutheran, we were not allowed to have a mass. Therefore, we Catholics in the family went to church in the morning and had a mass, and later on we had the wedding ceremony by itself. I was happy and promised Heinz never to bother him. So it was. Every Sunday, Heinz went to his church and I to mine. The children were baptized in the Catholic faith. Heinz came along.

I had a cleaning woman. One day, she came and asked me if I could do her a favor. She was Catholic. She told me that she was divorced and remarried. The Catholic church did not allow a divorce and had excommunicated her from the church. Her children were never allowed to be baptized. They were born within her second marriage. She was living in sin in the eyes of the Catholic Church and wanted to get out. "Please, can you write to the Pope and ask him to help me? I do not have the writing skills," she asked me. I felt for her, having been through only a little bit of her problem. The Pope was a little bit too far-fetched, but what about talking to a local priest? Well, here I had a problem again. I was not able to have a Catholic priest come over. I told her my misery. I made an arrangement for her with the priest of the church. In those days, he was not able to help her either.

There is one Catholic priest I still admire up to this day. Kirsten was born nine months and six days after we got married, Ingo twenty-two months after Kirsten. I think I would have had baby after baby. Being a perfectionist and overdoing everything, I was always too busy. When I had only Kirsten, I was busy with her the whole day. Having two children, I became a nervous nut. They had discovered the anti-baby pill. Being Catholic, I was not allowed to take it. When I went to confession, I told the priest my problem, that I would like to take the pill, but… This priest was very young. His answer was: "You alone have to decide to take the pill. Nobody can tell you what to do. You alone will one day stay in front of God, and you have to be responsible for your doings in life." I was relieved and took the pill. During my whole life, I was thankful to this priest and never ever forgot him. It shows how one priest can change the life of a person.

There are women who are born to enjoy lots of children and can handle it, but I realized early on that I did not have this capability. I tried so hard to raise my two children, read all the books, and yet I did make so many mistakes. Today, I am enjoying my two with all my heart. Where would I be without that priest?

Moving to the US was great. People were more religious. As I mentioned before, my first American girlfriend, Mary Frances, had nine children. How did she do it? Most families who became our friends had more than two children. In Germany, people had one child in those days; two was a lot, and people looked down on you. I asked myself: If I would have been raised in the US, would I have been able to have more children? The whole attitude was different. We lived in the New York metropolitan area, and most of our friends were Italian Catholics or Irish Catholics. Nobody was judged for being religious—just the opposite. Everybody was active in church. I felt very good. Being a perfectionist and an analyzer, I looked around to see how my friends did it. They had priorities. The children came first. The house was not important and could be messy. For me, the German, that was hard to do; but in the long run, I learned that attitude was more important than my outlook on life. I felt a real contrast between my upbringing in Germany and the American way of life. God and family were more important then things and cleaning.

I felt good being able to go to church without being looked down on either. My friend Mary Frances—the one with the 9 children— was almost like my grandmother. She went to mass every morning and made the sign of the cross, when she passed the church or a cross. I had not seen that since my grandmother died.

One neighbor was of German descent. She was second-generation. Her parents started a deli in Queens after they emigrated from Germany. She was happy when we Germans moved next to her. It was Helen. I have mentioned her before. She used to be Lutheran, but converted to the Catholic faith because her husband Jack was Irish, third-generation. After a couple of months, she invited us over for dinner. Well, she thought doing us a favor by inviting a Catholic priest of German descent. He was teaching at a nearby seminar. She did not know what she did to us. I was surprised: Heinz liked this Father Hendricks. He did not object to a Catholic priest. We had a nice conversation and a great evening.

Heinz got acquainted with all the Catholics around us. The children and I went to the Catholic church and he went to the Lutheran. Waltraud, the German friend we met right at the beginning, was Lutheran too. She introduced Heinz to the Lutheran church, and sometimes they went together. Occasionally, Heinz took Kirsten and Ingo along. I felt very guilty. I had to raise the children Catholic. After more than thirty years, when Kirsten was an adult, she told me that she liked the Lutheran church more than the Catholic. Everyone was happier and not so serious, and she still remembered that I cried and was sad when she went with her daddy to the Lutheran church. Again, I felt very guilty.

One year after we had met Father H. at Helen's house, we went to the Avery Fisher Hall in Manhattan for a concert. Looking back a couple of rows, there was this face which looked familiar. He was sitting between two women. I asked Heinz to turn around and see if he knew who it was. Then it hit us. It was Father H., whom we had met at Helen's dinner party. During intermission, we went to him. He did not recognize us. When we introduced ourselves, he remembered. The two ladies who were with him were two nuns. We had a nice little talk. Then he invited us to the seminar for a Christmas concert. The seminar was only fifteen minutes away from where we lived. Thankfully, we accepted this invitation. Three weeks later was Christmas. Heinz even wanted to go.

This concert turned our world around. After the concert, Father H. came with another priest to our table and introduced Father G. to us. Father G. had studied in Austria and got his PhD. in Trier, Germany. He spoke German and was happy to meet us. We had a nice talk, and then he asked Heinz some questions about the publisher in Germany who had published his thesis. I did not believe my ears. Heinz invited him over to our house to discuss this. What a change. I was excited. I asked Father G. what kind of food he liked. He liked Germany very much, and so he liked German food. He liked "tongue in Madeira." I promised him to prepare this for him when he came over. I would have cooked everything for him. This was a meal we had at our wedding dinner, at our reception. It was a very special one in Germany. When he came, I had invited our neighbors Helen and Jack too for dinner. They gave me a compliment and asked what it was. When they heard it was tongue, they stopped eating and did not touch the meat anymore.

Another event happened this evening. In Germany, you always address someone with all the titles. When Helen and Jack came in, they said, "Hallo Charlie" to Father G.. I had made place cards, which said "Professor Dr. G" Charlie—Dr. G.—laughed when he saw that and told Helen and Jack "Look that's what the Germans do."

From that moment on, Charlie became our best friend. He loved to come over for dinner, and I tried to cook what he liked. He was a gourmet. We had great conversations, and Heinz was all of a sudden very open-minded. Actually, Charlie and Heinz became real friends. What a change. We went together to concerts, plays, and often to mass at the seminar. Over the weekend, he was helping out at another parish. We went to mass over there. Yes, Heinz went with me to mass.

Later on, when I was working, Charlie came over very often to see Heinz and keep him company. They cooked together and talked, talked, talked. They became buddies. Quite often I served "tongue in Madeira."

After years of friendship, one day I was working again and called home from Florida to talk to Heinz when he told me that Charlie was over and they were enjoying themselves. Then I heard a sentence I will never forget, and it turned our world around. He told me, "I will convert to the Catholic faith."

"Did I hear right? Can you please repeat this?" I asked him. He did. And so it happened. Heinz converted to the Catholic faith. Charlie was the priest who prepared him, taught him, and did the ceremony. Heinz did it for the children, so that all four of us belonged to one denomination to celebrate together, especially first communion and confirmation of the children.

When Kirsten and Ingo had their first communion, we had a mass at home. We invited all our friends, Charlie celebrated the mass, and the children received their first communion by him. Afterwards, we had a great party. This was the same with their confirmation. Again, when Charlie confirmed Kirsten and two years later Ingo, we had a mass in our home surrounded by all our friends.

Charlie came over often for dinner and to other parties we had. He liked our friends and they liked him. He actually once gave Heinz and me a break. He babysat for Kirsten and Ingo over a whole weekend. We went to Montauk, Long Island, and enjoyed the ocean and ourselves while Charlie spoiled the children.

One thing happened to me now that Heinz was Catholic. I did not feel the responsibility as hard as before anymore to raise the children in the Catholic faith. We both were responsible. That felt very good.

When I started to work, I started with small jobs. I did city tours in Manhattan every Saturday and Sunday. This was good, because Heinz was home for the children. The tours were from nine a.m. to one p.m. I had to leave the house around seven-thirty a.m., when everybody was asleep. On the weekend, it took me around thirty minutes to get into midtown Manhattan. Often, I did night tours too. This all meant one thing. For the first time in my life, I had to skip going to church on Sunday. Heinz went with the children while I was gone. In the beginning, I felt very guilty. It was a sin. But through the years, my guilt disappeared. When the children were older, I liked to go during the week to mass at St. Patrick's, not to make up, but to enjoy mass on my own terms. Heinz went to church more then I did. I think I grew and did not feel the guilt anymore. At first it was my job which gave me the excuse, but then it was my inner feeling. I prayed a lot on my own terms too.

Once, I was in Manhattan with a girlfriend. We went to the Lutheran Church of St. Peter in the Citicorp Building. We even received communion from the Lutheran priest, and I did not feel guilty. The opposite—I felt as close to God as in the Catholic Church. How could this be a sin, as I thought and learned when I was young?

Being born in the thirties and raised in the forties and fifties, Catholicism was more about following impossible, nit-picking, spirit-numbing rules than it was about belief. We were discouraged from reading the Bible, which could only be filtered through priests, and we were in a perpetual state of sin because we believed what the nuns in their scary outfits taught us. Entering a Protestant church, you were condemned to purgatory, a temporary hell where your veins would turn to rivers of fire, and no matter how hard you screamed and cried and begged in agony, mercy would not rain down. Not until you'd completed your sentence, which would take eons, would you finally be admitted to an eternity of bliss in heaven. Unless, of course, you'd murdered someone or divorced and remarried or had sex without being married—then you were doomed to the pit of fire forever.

I was guilt-ridden and not a happy person. Coming to America gave me the freedom to explore my own soul. Sure, there were a lot of Catholic friends still around me, which felt good but I started to search the field. Nobody judged me or gave me advice or told me I was on the wrong track, as would have happened in Germany.

Before I started to work, I went once a week into Manhattan with a girlfriend while the children were in school. Around three p.m. we were back home. We visited the museum, went to the Avery Fisher Hall to listen to a rehearsal concert and met Leonard Bernstein this way, or only strolled around and felt the spirit of New York We always had lunch afterwards. One day we went to Barnes & Noble on Fifth Avenue and browsed around to see what new books were on the market. One book I saw which fascinated me. I started to read and was not able to stop. It was *The Power of Your Subconscious Mind* by Dr. Joseph Murphy. It was published 1963, and now it was 1976. It was as if he talked directly to me. In the foreword, he wrote, "Do you know the answers? Why is one man sad and another man happy? Why is one man joyous and prosperous and another man poor and miserable? Why is one man fearful and anxious and another full of faith and confidence? Why does one man have a beautiful, luxurious home while another man lives out a meager existence in a slum? Why is one man a great success and another an abject failure? Why is one speaker outstanding and immensely popular and another mediocre and unpopular? Why is one man a genius in his work or profession while the other man toils and moils all his life without doing or accomplishing anything worthwhile? Why is one man healed of a so-called incurable disease and another isn't? Why is it that so many good, kind, religious people suffer the tortures of the damned in their mind and body? Why is it that many immoral and irreligious people succeed and prosper and enjoy radiant health? Why is one woman happily married and her sister very unhappy and frustrated?

Is there an answer to these questions in the workings of your conscious and subconscious minds? There most certainly is."

Wow—this was it. These were all my questions in life. This was what I was trying to find out. I read this book, not once, but quite often. I not only read it, I practiced to change my thinking and living. I found the terms "conscious" and "subconscious" mind. My conscious mind is my brain and my subconscious mind is my soul. God gave me my soul and it is a part of God. I am a part of God. I am God's child. He loves me. "A knowledge of the interaction of your conscious and subconscious minds will enable you to transform your whole life," Murphy wrote and even more. "If your thought is in harmony with the creative principle of your subconscious mind, you are in tune with the innate principle of harmony. If you entertain thoughts which are not in accordance with the principle of harmony, these thoughts cling to you, harass you, worry you, and finally bring about disease, and if persisted in, possibly death. The Kingdom of happiness is in your thought and feeling."

On page 166, he writes: "God is the highest and best in you. Express more of God's love, light, truth, and beauty, and you will become one of the happiest persons in the world today."

He too urged people to pray. Prayers evoke miracles.

What a revelation! His book was the beginning of my change. I started to read more and more books. Some of the next ones were *The Power of Positive Thinking, The Power of Positive Living,* **and** *The Amazing Results of Positive Thinking* **by Norman Vincent Peale Pastor of the Marble Collegiate Church in Manhattan on Fifth Avenue. I went to lectures and became hungry for a more fulfilled life with love and happiness. From believing in the punishing God, I discovered a loving God, or Higher Power, or whatever you call** *Him* **who was filled with love and watched over me. I stopped going to confession. I did not feel like that sinner anymore. I was God's child, protected by him. I gave up praying the way I used to do it, out of guilt. I prayed a lot more. It became a conversation with God. I told him everything and believed in him, which led me to believing in myself.**

From the beginning of my youth, it made me think: "Why am I so lucky to be born in the only right faith?" What about all the other Religions or Denominations? Was it luck to be born into the only right church on earth? I bought a book, *Religions of the World,* and studied it. Now I reached the point I was looking for. My eyes and heart opened up to greater belief and joy. I learned more.

Through all religions, God shows himself to us. He gives us help to understand him through prophets. In the Christian faith, it was Jesus who called himself son of God, but we all are God's children. It was Mohamed in the Moslem faith. Shakyamuni Gautama became the Buddha in Buddhism. God shows his face in the teaching of the ancient Toltecs. Here, I read all three books by Don Miguel Ruiz, who was a healer. Through all religions and all the teachers of the world, God preaches and shows us Love is the only way to him. He shows himself through different religions, which meet different people's needs. One saying they all have: God is positive! There is nothing negative about him. If I am going to live God's way and am the person he wants me to be, I must line up my vision with his and learn to live in only a positive frame of mind. Learn to look for the best in every situation of my life. If I align my thoughts with God's thoughts and I start dwelling on the promises of his word, when I constantly dwell on thoughts of his victory, favor, faith, power, and strength, nothing can hold me back. When I think positive, excellent thoughts, I will be propelled toward greatness, inevitably bound for increase, promotion, and God's supernatural blessings. All religions taught this in different languages.

The Catholic Church was not the only church who taught the only right religion, as I was brought up to believe. How was it during the Middle Ages? Popes, priests, and all the emperors in Europe stuck together against the little people. They were very powerful and wanted more power by suppressing the people. They made people feel guilty. People were not free. The Inquisition was the police of the Catholic Church. How much misbehavior was done by it! So many people were persecuted by the church. There was no love. People obeyed out of fear.

Galileo Galilei (1564-1642), whom I admired, was in 1633 convicted by the Inquisition and sentenced to life imprisonment because he stuck to his discovery that the earth revolves around the sun and other planets. The sun, and not the earth, is the center of our system. Sure, he was allowed to serve his term under house arrest at his villa outside Florence. But he was excommunicated from the church, which must have been very hard for him. After hundreds of years, in the twentieth century, the Catholic church reversed his excommunication. What a sad story.

I never allowed myself to question the history of the church. I was afraid to do so, even today in our times. It would have been a sin. I became that guilt-ridden neurotic with a deep-in-my-bones conviction of my own badness. By studying all the other religions, I realized they all preach the same: "God is love." Only when man-made doctrines come in, we are in trouble. Realizing God is love and he created us in his image, I felt happier and happier.

I had a lot of questions. Many were answered when I started to believe in reincarnation. It made so much more sense. One question which I never had answered, being a strict Catholic, was: Why do we have on this earth some people who do only bad things, like murderers, thieves, child molesters, etc., and on the other hand people like Mother Theresa, Gandhi, or Francis of Assisi, whom I really adore? Why are some children born with great talents, like Mozart? Believing in reincarnation, I got the answer. Some people had lived through more and others through fewer lives. Some people had old souls, some were very young. Some people brought their talents from former lives into their next life, like Mozart and many others. I started to believe that we grow with each life more towards God and become one with him. Love is the road to God.

Being born is no accident. God created me, and there is a reason for all that is happening in my life. I have only to approach the questions in my life with a sense of faith and trust. I always have to be compassionate. My subconscious mind has a life of its own, which is always moving toward harmony, health, and peace. Knowing this made me feel happy, free from guilt. It turned my life around. Yet I had a lot of work to do. Changing is not easy. Heinz, who always let me be myself, was a big help, and my new home country, where I did not get judged, set me free to grow.

I used to be ridden with fear; what did I learn? Fear is the worst and takes you away from love. When the children were growing up, I always was afraid something would happen to them. My Irish girlfriend with nine children never was afraid that something would happen to her children. She put them into God's hands. They became happy adults. I am blessed; Kirsten and Ingo did not suffer under my guilt-ridden fear too much. Heinz was the one who gave them more self-confidence.

I have to repeat myself again and again: I was a very frightened woman! When we moved to Houston, we bought a contemporary house with lots of windows. Our bedroom was on the first floor. I always was used to having the bedroom on the second floor. One late afternoon, I went over to a neighbor to visit with her, because I was alone. Heinz was on a business trip. It was October and getting dark early. When I went back home, she teased me, "Shall I walk you home?"

"I am a big girl," was my answer, and we laughed. Coming home, I closed the blinds, put on the alarm, and went into my bathroom, when the doorbell rang. I was wondering who that might be. Was it my next-door neighbor, Arnette, whom I had just visited? I walked towards the front door. I had a very funny feeling. Walking from the bathroom into my bedroom, I saw the intercom right next to my bedroom door. My bedroom door was only ten feet away from the front door, and I never had used the intercom—didn't even know how it worked. My inner voice was so strong. I pushed a button, not knowing which one it was, and asked, "Who is it?"

I was surprised when I heard the voice of a man: "Ah. Ah," (stuttering), "this is Mr. Smith."

I did not know any Mr. Smith, so I asked, "What do you want?"

His answer: "Oh, I must be at the wrong house."

My bedroom door was so near at the front door that I heard his voice even without the intercom, and I heard him leaving. At first, I thought someone really was lost and picked the wrong house. But then it hit me, and I got scared. I called the police. They warned me to take precautions, to be alert, and not to open the front door if this happened again, but to call them right away. Like I said, I never had used the intercom, and I found out it only works when the main outlet in the kitchen is on. I had it on because I was listening to the radio. I became so calm; now I saw and felt that I was saved by my guardian angel. God had protected me. From that time on, I never was afraid to be by myself in our house.

Another time, I saw God's guidance. I had been with a German group for two weeks and had checked them in at Kennedy Airport to fly back home. My tour was over, and I was really happy. Everything had worked well, and my guests went home joyful and thankful. I too was looking forward to going home to Heinz and the children. I took the "train to the plane" from Kennedy Airport into the World Trade Center. I was carrying a couple of thousand dollars with me, which I had collected from the people during our trip for different special events. I had in mind to go to my agency the next day to settle my account and drop off the money. Arriving down underneath the WTC, I had to take the Path to New Jersey. When I left the train, I was the only person around. It was around eight p.m. and all the people working in downtown Manhattan had left for home. I had to change platforms. All of a sudden, someone else came down the staircase to my platform. He was an African American. I was on one side of the platform, walking towards the staircase; he was on the other side of the platform, walking towards me. I thought to myself, "I am safe. He is on the other side." When he was close to me, he switched and walked towards me, right in front of me. He went with his hand into the pocket of his jacket. I never found out what he wanted to get out of it. I do not know what happened, but I smiled at him and asked in German "How are you doing today?" This must have confused him, and he turned around. Maybe he thought someone was staying behind him or whatever; I do not know. But I saw three people coming down the staircase. He too saw these people and left. He did not bother me anymore. Then I started to shake. I went out of the subway system to safer ground and called Heinz to pick me up. He did. Again, God had saved me. I realized that God loves me, and I am protected. It gave me such a very good feeling.

God showed me his love quite often. Just last year, I had another experience. Every morning, I walk around the neighborhood, four to five miles. I walk through the path where no houses are. I am very cautious. But I walk through neighborhoods too.

One morning, I walked by a house in a neighborhood of houses. It was an intersection, and opposite of this house lived an older couple, whom I had seen often and we always said "Hallo." Walking by one of the houses opposite of this couple's house, I heard, "Hallo, hallo." I looked around and saw a guy on the roof. He looked good, like my next-door neighbor. "Would you please help me?" he asked. "My ladder fell down and I cannot get off this roof. Would you please go into the back yard and pick up the ladder? The gate right there should be open!"

I saw the gate at the fence. It was right next to the street. I told him "Okay."

Well, the gate was locked. Then he told me, "Please come through the garage into the kitchen, which will lead you into the back yard." I had a funny feeling, but it was my neighbor, even though I did not know him and never saw him. We only lived three blocks away. I went into the garage opened the door to whatever it was. There was a computer, and on the screen was porno—a naked woman lying there with her legs stretched out and her breasts up.

I was shocked, closed the door, and went back out. I did not see the man and called, "Hallo, hallo." I intended to tell him that I was not coming in, but that I would call a neighbor for him to help him. There was no answer anymore, and nobody was on the roof anymore. I left very fast and went home to tell Heinz. We went to the police and reported this incident. The police sent a patrol officer over to check him out. We learned he was a teacher at a high school home for spring break. He had all kind of excuses when the officer questioned him. He is on the police watch list now. Again I was saved! I have a guardian angel.

These were very drastic moments when I got saved and I saw God's guidance.

In my daily life, I was very shy and scared too. I recall when I started to work, I was afraid of the people who came over. They had paid a lot of money for this trip, and I was expected to perform and give them the best of the best. I was very scared in the beginning when I started to work. I will never forget when I picked up people from the airport. I did not look at them, but sat in the front seat, talking into the microphone and looking straight ahead at the highway. Once, I even gave my seat away to stand down next to the driver on the steps of the bus where nobody could see me. Through the years, I became more confident and loved to talk to people looking into their eyes. I saw so much love coming back to me, which made me more and more confident. I became myself. The more I became myself, the more people liked me. They saw my potential, which I never had seen in myself. Through their eyes, I started to see it and started to love myself.

I realized I started to draw people to me who where struggling with the same growing-up pain I was.

In the very beginning, I had a group of architects who came to the USA to study all the modern skyscrapers built by Philip Johnson, Gropius, Mies van der Rohe and Frank Lloyd Wright and Le Corbusier. It was the beginning of the 1980s, the very first years of my job. I had a professor on the bus from NYU and had only to translate what he was saying. One architect, who was in charge of the whole group, brought his wife along. Something did get connected between us. We found out we were searching for the same things. She recommended the books of Gustav Freitag, which she had read and which turned her thinking around. We learned that Gustav Freitag was a scholar of Dr. Joseph Murphy, exactly the one whose book I read in the very beginning. Today, I know the same energy we both experienced brought us together.

I loved my opera-groups. Usually, people were older and allowed themselves in these expensive tours after they had established a good life. One exception was a young woman who came over and over again. Her name was Eva, and I liked her very much. We got drawn together again by a higher power. She too was changing. Born in Austria, she belonged to the last royal family before it became a democracy. As I mentioned before, the aristocrats still today think they are superior. She was never allowed to become herself. She was supposed to live like an aristocrat. One love she had; it was music. Her father demanded from her at least to get her Ph.D. She did it for her father. She got her doctoral degree in music. This was the reason that she attended opera tours. On these trips we found each other, even though we were from different societies. She was all the way up there, and I came from the middle class. But one thing we had in common: we both were searching for our inside. In Europe, it counts what society you are born in and you stay there. In the USA, you can become yourself. We both were trying to find out who we are and why we are on this earth. We read books together. I still recall one time. We were at the St. Francis Hotel in San Francisco. Eva came over to my room, and we sat together and read Gustav Freitag's book. It felt so good to find someone struggling the same way I did. She gave her life more meaning. Ten years ago, she adopted a very disturbed little girl from a third-world country and now gives her all the love to turn this little girl's life around to a better one. But her music is still her second love. She founded a private music center in Vienna. We are still very fond of each other today and can exchange our inner thoughts. The search for a meaningful life and the power of God brought us together.

It became amazing for me how I got drawn to people with the same thoughts. This was not an accident, but God's gift to strive towards him to the light. Who is God? As a child, I pictured him as a man, but he is the *alpha est. et o,* the energy of love, the everything we cannot picture but believe in and feel him. I got to know more and more people who believed this. We were drawn towards each other. But one thing I realized: people from Germany and Austria who were on this journey were different. I learned they were not able to share their thoughts with people around them. They were alone, because it was still a new belief system for average people, and they got judged. They did not fit in. They must be very strong to take this journey, while here in USA I had back-up from quite a lot of friends. Here, we could develop ourselves in each direction. Even Oprah had on her show Gary Zukav or Marianne Williamson and my newest friend, Joel Osteen.

I started not to believe in this punishing God anymore, but the God of love. Even more, my fear was disappearing. I got up in the morning happier and happier, looking forward to the day and thanking God for letting me be and letting me grow. My prayers were not anymore the ones out of fear and obedience, but of happiness and love. I talked to him and enjoyed my walks every morning where I was not interrupted by noises of the outside world, but enjoyed his nature.

Looking inside myself, I felt happiness more and more. What did Dr. Murphy say? "The great things of life are simple, dynamic, and creative. They produce well-being and happiness." St. Paul reveals to us how we can think our way into a life of dynamic power and happiness in these words: "Finally brethren, whatsoever things are true, whatsoever things are honest, whatsoever things are just, whatsoever things are pure, whatsoever things are lovely, whatsoever things are of good report; if there be any virtue, and if there be any praise, think on these things" (Philippians 4:8).

Happiness was always far away for me. I had to perform as a child, as a wife, as a mother. I still recall how, as children, my sister and I were laughing at the dinner-table and were told to stop it. The more we were told to stop it, the more we had to laugh. Our mother at one point told us "Time out. Each of you stand in one corner." We got punished for being happy.

Growing up during the war and after the war when we had nothing, I thought happiness would come by owning artificial things. To this day, I have an opera record. On the front page is a lady in a long evening gown, and a gentleman is helping her into a fur coat. This was my dream as a young girl: to become someone like that. I mentioned it before: I got the fur coat, not one but a couple. I wore evening gowns when we went to functions, but these things did not bring happiness into my life. Real happiness comes from inside.

I realized one thing. What you put into your mind will come through. What did Marcus Aurelius, the great Roman philosopher, say? "A man's life is what his thoughts make of it." Emerson, America's foremost philosopher, said, "A man is what he thinks all day long." I wanted to go to operas. I had to go when I was very young and did not understand it, but through that I found the love for operas. When we came to America, I thought I never would be able to work if something happened to Heinz. In my mind, you had to be very educated to find a job in this country. My education was from Germany, and I thought that did not count at all. I did not know in those days that most Americans came into this country to find work and find a better life. Well, in my thoughts, I was afraid.

As I had mentioned before, I loved operas, and when we came over, Maria Callas was supposed to appear herself in one opera. It was a dream come true for me. I only had read about her. Now it became reality. These were my feelings too when I went to the Metropolitan Museum of Art. Paintings I only knew from my books. Now the originals were hanging there in front of me. It was overwhelming. Well, going back to the Met, I never heard or saw Maria Callas. The Met was closed because there was a strike. But when it opened again, we went and saw *The Girl of the Golden West* with Renate Tebaldi. This was my first experience with the Met. I was overwhelmed again. I did not believe it. I had to pinch myself. It was a highlight. During intermission, I went to the powder room.

There was a lady who cleaned the toilets, and I thought to myself, as I mentioned before, "If anything should happen to Heinz, I can become a toilet lady. This way I could always can hear operas." I put this into my mind, but greater things happened. When I started to work and got opera groups, I not only went constantly to the Met in Manhattan, but flew with the people to the Lyric Opera in Chicago and to the Memorial Opera in San Francisco and had people around me to talk about this. America was not what I thought it was. I learned that if you have a dream, you are able to fulfill it. You are even able to fulfill it to the greatest. My thoughts—everybody's thoughts—will always become reality. I experienced the American Dream.

I had another vision or dream. I wanted to communicate with people. I wanted to write a book. After all my tours, I became very friendly with people, and they liked me. You remember how afraid I always was before I started a tour? But afterwards, I was on cloud nine when I came home. I got nice letters where people told me how great I was and how much I gave them, especially how they got a real idea about American living and the American people. Hearing this over and over again for nineteen years made me very happy and gave me more self-esteem. Quite a lot of people told me during the years to write a book and let other people know "the American way of life." In the beginning, I turned this idea down and thought, "How am I able to do so?" But through the years, the idea grew. After I stopped working, it became a vision of mine. I saw it in my mind how this book became reality. One day I sat down and did it. I constantly talked to God about it and got a good feeling and ideas while I was walking through God's nature in the morning. I saw the book coming out as a bestseller in bookstores all over Germany. The title was *Between Two Worlds: A German Girl Discovers*

America. It was written in German for German people. I found a publisher in Germany, and yes, it was available all over Germany and even through "Amazon.de." I was thrilled and happy. I got phone calls from people I had never met who liked my book. One woman told me her son is married in the USA to an American girl, and she often visits them, and through my book she learned why they do what they are doing and why they are what they are. There are different ways of life in these two countries. I learned that one teacher made his class buy the book and he taught the class about the American way of life though it. I got a lot of other positive reactions. Sure, there must have been people who did not like it or did not believe in it, but I did not hear from them. My vision became reality. I thanked God. An American editor to whom I gave my book first before I found this German publisher told me to write another book. "God gave you this gift." That was too much for me. I laughed and turned the idea down.

Then the big disappointment came along. My publisher was a crook. He had printed my book and displayed it to bookstores, but he never advertised it or marketed it otherwise. It only sold through word-of-mouth recommendations from people who liked it. The book had a lot of bad grammar, even though it was edited before he got it. Then I learned from people who wanted to buy it that it was not available in bookstores anymore. I became more and more disappointed. I was not the only one he harmed. There were authors in Germany who had given him money, and he even never published their books. He got sued by a lot of people and had to close his office. My book disappeared from the market. I never learned how many books he had sold for me, because he pocketed the money. I did not believe this. Here I had this great vision and believed in God that it would become reality, and then I got so disappointed. But I did not give up. I prayed and thanked God anyhow, knowing He had more or better things to come. Today, I know it. I never would have started to write this book. I never would have searched more and more, as I did when this book grew in my mind. He leads us his way where we are able to grow more and more.

When I was a child and read all the biographies of the saints, I admired them. I believed in all the miracles I read about. How the mother of God appeared in Lourdes and Fatima to those children. I envied them. I never thought that God would have miracles for me. That was too far-fetched. I thought that miracles were only for the chosen ones, not for me. The more I got away from the obligation of the church and got more drawn towards God, the more I realized God's miracle towards me.

When I started my job, I was not able to choose trips. I was happy with what my agency gave me. I got a two-week-long bus tour through New England into Canada and back through New York, Pennsylvania, and Washington, DC, into New York City. There was a lot to study. I did it every night for the next day. Every morning when I started, I was filled with fear. There were thirty-something people watching me perform. Before I left my hotel room, I prayed very hard, persuading God to help me. I had to give city tours in all the large cities, had to teach about the country and the people. How was I able to do that? But a miracle happened. I talked and talked and talked. I was surprised at myself. I didn't believe it. Not only did I talk—no, what I told my tourists was brilliant and very interesting. I did not know how I was able to do this. Yes, I learned it. God inspired me. He gave me the gift and knowledge to perform like this. The people were very happy with me and told me how knowledgeable I was. Coming back to my hotel room at night,

I thanked God because I realized it was not me. He put this into me. It was a miracle or, better said, my miracle. I overcame the fear because I learned to trust him. Out of this trust, I took on longer trips where I had to learn more and more, and he always was on my side and made not only me happy but my people too.

This was when I began to believe in miracles. I trusted God. One time, I had a very important group of CEO's of German companies. Everything was the best of the best. We were in the most expensive hotels, ate at the best restaurants. One day, I had to do an evening dinner cruise on the Potomac River in Washington, DC, with them. Again, a five-star hotel was chosen close to the departure point, so that we were able to walk to the place where our boat departed from. They wanted to walk. Everything was great. We had a very nice evening. Then, suddenly, before our boat trip ended, it started to rain. It not only rained, it poured down from heaven. I was in shock. What should I do to get them back to the hotel without them becoming soaking wet? They were such important people. I knew there were not enough cabs around where we were ending our boat trip. I was not able to call anyone. Cellular phones were not around either. I *prayed;* what else could I do? I prayed very hard. Gold helped me again. When we got off the boat, there was a city bus sitting there with a driver. I excused myself, ran over to the bus, and told the driver my dilemma. I begged him to drive us over to the hotel, when I would give him fifty dollars. He had thirty minutes till his next job came around. When he heard he could make fifty dollars, he agreed. He drove over to pick up my people. They did not believe it, how friendly American people were and how everything over here worked so easily. How people helped each other. I did not tell them about the money I gave the bus driver, but I sent a Big "Thank you" to God.

Another fear I overcame: driving onto a highway, I was scared. For years now, it happens every time when I drive onto a highway that there are no cars coming. I always have enough space to get on, and then cars are coming again. Isn't that a help from God? Heinz is my witness. He always watches it with me now. It took me a long time to realize how God was protecting me and taking away my fear.

I had a slipped disc and sometimes I was in terrible pain. One thing I had learned through reading all my books was that at least 80% of all sickness of the body starts by burying Hurt and pain deep in our hearts or in our subconscious minds. We are pushing negative thoughts and actions down by being hurt from the outside world. All my fear of life I used to have ended up giving me back problems.

Again, I have to quote Dr. Murphy. He wrote: "When mentally disturbed the best procedure is to let go, relax, and still the wheels of your thought processes. Speak to your subconscious mind, telling it to take over in peace, harmony and divine order. You will find that all the functions of your body will become normal again. If you completely entrusted yourself to its wonder-working power, you would be entirely restored to health."

A classical instance of the Bible is recorded in Matthew 9:28-30: "And when he was come into the house, the blind men came to him: and Jesus saith unto them, Believe ye that I am able to do this? They said unto him, Yea, Lord. Then touched he their eyes, saying, according to your faith be it unto you. And their eyes were opened; and Jesus straitly charged them, saying, see that no man know it."

In the words, "According to your faith be it unto you," we can see that Jesus was actually appealing to the cooperation of the subconscious mind of the blind men. Their faith was their great expectancy, their inner feeling, their inner conviction that something miraculous would happen, and that their prayer would be answered, and it was. This is the time-honored healing technique of healing by all healing groups throughout the world, regardless of religious affiliation. The more deeply you believe in God the Almighty, the more he will heal you.

Some years ago, Heinz and I flew to Lake Tahoe to go skiing. Again, I had terrible back pain. For years I had a slipped disk, and doctors told me they were not able to do anything. I knew what it was. This was the anger I had pushed down when I had hurt feelings. My slipped disk really acted up. On the way to the airport, I sat on my hands in the car so no movement would go into my back. From the parking lot, we took a little bus to the airport where I was standing. I was afraid to sit, because the suspension of the bus was terrible, and each move went into my back. Now I took over and did what I had learned and read and experienced. Why did I not pray very hard? From entering the plane till we arrived, I prayed over and over again "The perfection of God is now being expressed through me. He is now filling my subconscious mind with perfect health, harmony, peace, joy and abundance. These are continually flowing through me, vivifying, inspiring, and prospering me. God recreates my body in perfect accordance with the perfect image held in the mind of God."

A miracle happened. When we landed in Lake Tahoe and I got off the plane, I had no back pain anymore, and it did not come back. I thanked God from the depth of my heart. Heinz was very surprised. He saw me before and after. What a difference. It was my miracle. I experienced the miracles I always had longed for.

Yes, God took away more and more of my fear, and I became a happier person, believing in him and feeling protected by him. I was not alone anymore. If I did my work here on earth, he was there for me. That made me feel very good and happy. Where did I come from? I used to be this very fearful person and now I am this happy one. Thank you, God.

One thing I became to believe: our life is designated by God. When we are born, we are already born into a family which challenges us. There is a purpose for it. When we grow up, everything is meant to be. We only have to listen to God, to our inner voice. Today, I even believe that my mother died so early for me. I never would have gone to America. I never would have had the courage to tell her, "I am leaving you and taking your only two grandchildren with me." This took me a long time to find out, but looking back over my life, I really know it.

Therefore, I am taking from God what he gives me, even when it sometimes looks like it is not good at the moment. Last year, I had one given moment of this. April 2 was my birthday, and April 4 was our fortieth wedding anniversary. Heinz and I wanted to celebrate really nicely. We both love Mexico and have been over there quite often. The only nice place left to discover was Mancanillo. We booked ourselves into the nicest resort hotel, the Las Hadas. Yes, it was out of this world, built in the Moorish style, which I like very much. The first day, we enjoyed all the gorgeous facilities. We ate in the greatest rooftop restaurant, had our margaritas at the pool, watched the sunset and made plans for my birthday and our anniversary. We really hit it. This was the first of April.

On April 2, we went into town to see what this village is all about. Well, we did not make it very far. I slipped on the sidewalk and was unable to get up again. Here I lay in the hot sun of Mexico with my white pants in the dirt of the pedestrian way. Heinz tried franticly to get me up; no success. People gathered around me, police came, and within twenty minutes, they had called an ambulance. I was in terrible pain when they put me on a stretcher and drove me to the next hospital. Over there, I met a trauma specialist. He took x-rays, and another doctor, an orthopedist, came back to tell me that my femur bone was fractured and I needed surgery. "Happy birthday!"

The orthopedist recommended surgery done by himself and his father or being airlifted back to the United States. I was in such pain and wanted to get it over with. My questions were: "Have you done surgery like this before?" and "Are you able to do it right away?" He needed to check me out, needed to know my blood type and then get blood from Guadalajara, which was four hours away. Heinz and I agreed to have the surgery done by him and his father as soon as possible. It was a very small hospital, with only eight rooms, but open for the public twenty-four hours every day of the week. The father, himself a surgeon, had founded this hospital eleven years ago. It was the Centro Medico Quirurgico Echauri in Manzanillo, Mexico. I got a nice room with a couch where Heinz could sleep. I felt very good with my doctor. He was very concerned. His sister, a doctor herself who specialized as an internist, gave me a good check-up.

The next day, my doctor told me he and his father would do the surgery at seven at night. I asked him why at night, and he told me that it is very peaceful and not as hectic as during the day. There were four doctors. My doctor and his father, who did the surgery, an anesthetist, a radiologist, and a lot of nurses. The surgery was from seven p.m. to twelve a.m., exactly five hours. Back in my bed, I recovered fast. What really surprised me was my doctor; he came at least four to five times during the day, asking how I was, if I was in pain, etc. He really was there for me, even though he had so many outpatients. At one point, I asked him, "When do you sleep?" Very bashfully, he smiled. He was there for all his patients, no matter what time of the day it was. He was really dedicated to his "calling"; for him, it was not a job. At one point, he admitted that he loved what he was doing, and it showed.

After I stayed for six days in the hospital, I was released. We were able to keep our hotel room. My doctor showed me how to use crutches, but it was harder than it looked. I almost fell. I had told him that our hotel was very cozy for healthy people, but for me with crutches, it was scary because of the marble floor. We had a semi-suite with two steps down to the seating area and another two steps down to the bathroom. My doctor listened and disappeared. I thought he would get me a wheelchair and bring me to a cab. What happened still gives me goose bumps. He came back with his father, his sister, and an uncle. All the doctors put me on a stretcher and put me into their ambulance. The doctor father drove it, and all the doctors brought me from my hospital bed into my hotel room and put me on my bed over there. I could not believe this. Was that dedication or what? Leaving, my doctor checked out the room and the floor and told me, "You were right—it is dangerous. Be careful!"

The bandage and small cast had to be taken off after three to four days. I asked my doctor if he would be able to come to the hotel to do so. He promised to do this, but it would be Saturday (Easter) night around eleven p.m. or twelve a.m., because during the day he was too busy. On Saturday, we waited and waited, nothing happened. We called around twelve a.m. and were told the doctor was performing an emergency surgery, but he would be coming up to the hotel the next day, on Easter Sunday, around three p.m., and he did. He came with his sister (the internist), and both took off my bandages. We learned that there were a lot of accidents, and therefore he was so busy. He chatted with us for more than half an hour. Where do you find a doctor like this? To top it all was the bill. The whole surgery plus hospital-stay and medication cost us only $4,300.

Another joyful experience I had. We had to stay longer in the hotel than we thought to recover. It was Easter, and a lot of Mexicans were coming. But we were able to keep our room. The hotel management sent a fruit basket to my hospital to cheer me up. Back in the hotel, I had to sit in a chair. Every morning, the maid brought me a flower and English magazines people had left back in their room. She did not speak English and I did not speak Spanish, but it was a wonderful communication between the two of us.

When I came back to the States, I had to go to a follow-up doctor. He was surprised at what a good job the Mexican doctor had done. Everybody was surprised. When I was in Mexico, our Kirsten called daily, telling us to come back to the USA to have the surgery done in the US and not in Mexico. She had talked to US doctors who had told her how dangerous it is over there. One day, sitting in the waiting room of my follow-up doctor, a woman asked me what was wrong with me. I told her my story. She told me her story. She had had a hip replacement, and it went wrong. The doctor had to do it over again. Why did everybody think badly about Mexican doctors? There are good ones and bad ones all over. Because everybody felt so negative, I told my Mexican doctor to let people know in the USA. So I did. I send my little story to Dateline, 20/20, O-Magazine, the Houston Chronicle, and more. Nobody was interested in it. I thought, "They all bring negative stories from other countries; why not let people know about this?" But everybody I told my story to was telling me "You were lucky."

Back at home, people were sad that this happened to me on my fortieth anniversary and my birthday, but I think it was a blessing. God gave me a real gift. I looked into the hearts of so many beautiful people and saw their love, dedication, and compassion. Without my fall, Heinz and I would have celebrated our anniversary by eating, drinking, enjoying ourselves. But this way, I saw a deeper spiritual way of finding my soul in other souls—finding God's love and compassion.

If I mentioned this to friends, there were only very few who understood me. Most told me they would have preferred the other way of celebrating those events. Those who understood me were on their personal spiritual way, searching for God. For me, it was a great blessing—a gift from God.

Another sad thing—or, better said, learning process—happened to me. A couple of years ago, I picked up a suitcase and fractured two vertebrae. It was very painful, and I learned nothing could be done for it. They would heal again by themselves. This meant I was not able to move around or I was in terrible pain. I sat day and night in a wheelchair for three and a half months. One lesson I learned: to be patient. It was a big lesson, because usually I am not that way. If I got up, I had to move very carefully. One wrong move and I experienced terrible pain. Often I screamed out loud. I learned to sit in my chair and avoid moving. I read lots of books. After three and a half months, I started only slowly to do things. I only was able to do little things. I was happy to empty the dishwasher, bend down, and empty the washer and dryer. These were only little things, but I learned a big lesson. I was so thankful to God for each move I was able to do. Often, I called Heinz and showed him what I was up to doing again. Even today, after years, I count my blessings to be healthy and to do things I was not able to do for a long time. This would never have happened without this painful terrible sickness. Before, I took my health for granted. I never thought of being unable to do things. I am thankful to God that it happened to me and that he showed me the beauty of living without pain. Another miracle.

Growing up, I learned materialism is something bad. But I changed and learned the opposite. While I was working, I wanted to invest my money. It was such a good feeling to have my own money. It empowered me and Heinz let me do whatever I wanted. I decided to buy an apartment in Miami Beach. It was 1987, and Miami, even Miami Beach, was run down. Everybody told me not to invest in that part of the States, even Heinz. I had such a strong inner voice to buy it anyhow, and I listened. It is a one-bedroom apartment right on the ocean. God gave me strength to do so and told me. Today, it is worth around $300,000 and going up. I bought it for only $60,000.

Writing this book, I realize the blessing of coming to America. In Germany, I would have been discouraged to write or think like this. People would have laughed at me. Here, I am able to be what I am and to search for my inner soul. I do not get judged.

After all those years being away from Germany, I learned recently that people still judge one another and look down on lower classes, which I do not realize when I visit people in Germany. A couple of weeks ago, Heinz and I went for ten days to the Dominican Republic. I had always heard when I was working that it was such a nice island. In our resort, we were surrounded by German, French, and other European people. We saw three German planes at the airport when we arrived. We loved it very much. The beach was awesome. It was white pulverized sand with large palm trees. The resort was nice. It had seven restaurants.

Coming home, I called my sister in Germany and told her about all the German people. Her answer was: "Yes, all the lower-class people are flying into the Domrep" (that's the German given name for Dominican Republic). I recall in the 1950s, when we still lived in Germany, there was a trend to spend vacations in Majorca. It was very reasonable. I never would have spent vacation there either, because only the chambermaids—which meant the lower class of people—were going there. I recall I was a very snobbish German too. But now I realized how I had changed through my stay in the US. I told my sister: "You know, those low-class people know where it is nice, and all the ones who think this way and do not explore that beautiful island miss out on a lot." Other friends in Germany whom I told about it were very reserved, when they normally would say, "Wow." Now I knew why they were not thrilled about our vacation place. I was embarrassed that people still thought like this. I was even more embarrassed when I looked into my mirror. Years ago, in Germany, I had the same attitude and looked down on people. I am ashamed, but yes, I have changed and am free of this feeling. America has changed me a lot. I have been away from Germany too long, and, like I say, when I am there for vacation, I am not able to know how people think and feel. Everybody is nice to me. Another big awakening for being blessed to be where I am.

I never listened to preachers on television, but one or two years ago I got by accident a channel where a young preacher was on. I only got a couple of sentences from his sermon, but he caught me; I had to listen. His words touched my heart and my soul. It was Pastor Joel Osteen from Houston. Living in Houston, I think he was on a local channel, but he caught my attention. I listened not only one time; I looked him up in the television guide and listened every week. He was pastor of the non-denominational Lakewood Church for a couple of years, following in the footsteps of his father, who also was a preacher but had passed away, and he took over even though he had a totally different message. He was positive and touched the goodness in people. He is trying to take away the guilt we all have. He introduced a loving God and built up our self-esteem. He reminded me of Dr. Murphy. After listening to him for a while, a girlfriend from New York one day asked me on the phone if I knew Joel Osteen because he lived in Houston. I told her that I had been listening to him for a while. She and her husband too had him on every week and were happy to hear him. Joel Osteen had gone public in the meantime and was on various channels every Sunday all over the USA and other countries. Then our best friend, who now is a Monsignor in the Catholic Church—I mentioned him before, Charlie—told me that he had heard from him and had listened to his television sermon. He liked him.

Living so close to this preacher, I became anxious to see and experience his Lakewood parish. One Sunday, Heinz and I drove over, and there he was with his wife, mother, brother, and children. The church was packed, and everybody was so cheery. His sermon was again great, but the worship was a little bit too much for me, coming from a Catholic background. People were throwing their hands and arms around. It reminded me of the Baptist church in Harlem. When I was working, I gave a lot of Harlem tours which ended in the Metropolitan Baptist Church on 128th Street, where we attended a Sunday sermon. Here, too, at first I felt a little bit strange, but through the years, I liked it more and more, and I got to know a couple of people. Being German and being Catholic, this was a revelation. As a German girl, I was raised not to show my feelings. I was not the only one. Here, they showed their inner feelings and let those out.

Again, I have to go back to my opera groups when I was working. In one group, I had a man who was retired and loved operas. He had been a very well-known and famous district attorney in Munich. He was from the old school a real male chauvinist. Once, his wife came along. She had nothing to say, but she catered to him and did everything he said—or better, demanded. The first time I had him in my group, I got scared. He put down everybody. It was hard to please him. In these opera groups, there were usually very educated people. If there were female attorneys or medical doctors, he looked down on them and even said nasty words. As a start, we always had a cocktail reception, where I had to welcome everybody and we all had to get to know each other better. He was very rude. He talked down to people and upset them, especially those women. Thirteen times he came to New York, almost every year. Through the years, I got to know him better and better. After a couple of times seeing him, I was not afraid of him anymore, because I saw his inner core, which was very soft. I always knew what happened so I kept him away from targets he would upset: female professionals. Through the years, I gained his trust. One time, he asked me not to tell other people what he used to do for a living. I don't know why, but I think he was afraid that somebody would recognize him. I saw he was not free and himself.

After a couple of years, I had to give a Harlem tour to an opera group he was in. It was the first time he attended it. When we were at the Metropolitan Baptist Church attending the sermon, I did not believe what I saw. I was sitting next to Dr. Rudolf Samper. All of a sudden, he took my hand. I looked at him, and here he was crying. This tough guy was so greatly touched by all the feelings people let out. Afterwards, he asked me, "Why did you not bring me over here sooner?"

I have to tell more about him how softened he became. One day, he called me from Germany. He told me that he was very ashamed to attend another opera group, but he loved operas so much, and therefore he wanted to let me know why he was ashamed to come. He got divorced and was living together with a younger woman. In the meantime, he was close to eighty and this younger woman was sixty-four years old. He was very much in love. He asked me if I would be very upset. I assured him that I loved him the way he was and that I would be glad when I was him again. He did not attend any opera groups for years, and now I knew why. He was very happy to have this off his chest, and I was very happy to see him again and couldn't wait to see his girlfriend. I went to Kennedy Airport and picked up the group. I did not believe what I saw when he came out of customs. He had changed. I only knew him wearing expensive business suits. Now he was dressed in jeans, a very nice shirt, and a baseball hat. I had to hold my breath. We hugged like good old friends, and then a very attractive woman came smiling toward me. This was his girlfriend. She had really changed him. Checking them in at the hotel, I had to laugh again. He took me aside and whispered into my ear, "Ulla, please do not read out loud both of our names, because we are not married and nobody should know that we have a room together." He still was ashamed and not free to do what he wanted to do. We had a ball together on this tour. I really liked his girlfriend.

When we went to Lakewood Church, I thought of this Dr. Samper, how he had changed and how inspired he was. I think we German people are afraid of showing our feelings. Therefore, I did not feel too happy during the Lakewood sermon. It was a little bit too much for me. I still have a lot of German attitude and have trouble letting go and showing my feelings to the whole world, forgetting about what other people think. It is built into our system. I always felt good in Harlem, but this came through the years after I grew into it. I cannot judge the sermon at Lakewood Church. I really want to go back one day, and we will.

After reading Joel Osteen's book, I was happy and affirmed again that I was on the right path and why I was a much happier person than I used to be. I actually got some prayers out which were identically the same than Dr. Murphy's. Here they are both for the morning:

Osteen's: "Father, I'm excited about today. This is a day You have made; I'm going to rejoice and be glad in it. God, I know You reward those who seek You, so I thank You in advance for Your blessings, favor, and victory in my life today.

"Father, I thank you that I am strong in the Lord and the power of Your might. I am well able to do what You have called me to do."

Dr. Murphy's: "God, you take charge of my life today and every day. All things work together for good for me today. This is a new and wonderful day for me. There will never be another day like this one. I am divinely guided all day and whatever I do will prosper. Divine love surrounds me, enfolds me, and enwraps me, and I go forth in peace. Whenever my attention wanders away from that which is good and constructive, I will immediately bring it back to contemplation of that which is lovely and of good report. I am a spiritual and mental magnet attracting to myself all things which bless and prosper me. I am going to be a wonderful success in all my undertakings today. I am definitely going to be happy all day long."

These prayers are very helpful to me. I accept myself as a child of God and know he is with me and guides me. I know that he will bring out only the best in me. I do not feel like that terrible sinner anymore.

Where am I today?

Today, I am a happy and calm person. My fear and anxiety are gone. Every morning, I awake looking forward what the day will bring. My children both became great, responsible people. I adore them, and they adore me. I am proud of them, and we love each other very much.

Heinz and I live a very harmonious life. We both came with a lot of baggage but worked our way through it and made it. We enjoy being together twenty-four hours. We do not take each other for granted, but respect each other. Our love for each other grew and deepened. I can say he is my best friend. He let me become myself.

Through all the years, I learned so much and grew to be what I am today. As this book shows, I had to go a long way. I am looking forward to the future and cannot wait to see what is in stock for me. I embrace my life, which God gave me. I see all the gifts God bestowed on me and try to live by it, to come closer to him. But all this I would have not been able to do in Germany. There, I would have been a part of the society I lived in and would have tried to do what they asked me to do out of fear of being judged. Today, I say from the depth of my heart that I am proud to be a citizen of the

United States of America. I became a citizen very late. It was 1994, because before I wanted to die as a German citizen; but I learned what this country—my new home country—is all about and what it gave me. It is the greatest country in the world, where everybody can become him- or herself. It is the only country where it can happen. Therefore, I say:

THANKS, AMERIKA! YOU SET ME FREE.

www.ingramcontent.com/pod-product-compliance
Lightning Source LLC
Chambersburg PA
CBHW020246290526
45784CB00003B/1114